**OPPOSING
VIEWPOINTS®
SERIES**

D0376380

Medical Marijuana

Other Books of Related Interest

Opposing Viewpoints Series

Alternative Medicine
Marijuana

At Issue Series

Alcohol Abuse
Cancer
Health Care Legislation

Current Controversies Series

Medicare

"Congress shall make
no law … abridging
the freedom of speech,
or of the press."

First Amendment to the US Constitution

The basic foundation of our democracy is the First Amendment guarantee of freedom of expression. The Opposing Viewpoints Series is dedicated to the concept of this basic freedom and the idea that it is more important to practice it than to enshrine it.

**OPPOSING
VIEWPOINTS®
SERIES**

Medical Marijuana

Margaret Haerens and Lynn M. Zott, Book Editors

GREENHAVEN PRESS
A part of Gale, Cengage Learning

GALE
CENGAGE Learning·

Detroit • New York • San Francisco • New Haven, Conn • Waterville, Maine • London

Elizabeth Des Chenes, *Director, Publishing Solutions*

© 2013 Greenhaven Press, a part of Gale, Cengage Learning

Gale and Greenhaven Press are registered trademarks used herein under license.

For more information, contact:
Greenhaven Press
27500 Drake Rd.
Farmington Hills, MI 48331-3535
Or you can visit our Internet site at gale.cengage.com.

For product information and technology assistance, contact us at:

Gale Customer Support, 1-800-877-4253.
For permission to use material from this text or product, submit all requests online at www.cengage.com/permissions.

Further permissions questions can be emailed to permissionrequest@cengage.com.

Articles in Greenhaven Press anthologies are often edited for length to meet page requirements. In addition, original titles of these works are changed to clearly present the main thesis and to explicitly indicate the author's opinion. Every effort is made to ensure that Greenhaven Press accurately reflects the original intent of the authors. Every effort has been made to trace the owners of copyrighted material.

Cover Image © Thinkstock/Getty Images.

LIBRARY OF CONGRESS CATALOGING-IN-PUBLICATION DATA

Medical marijuana / Margaret Haerens and Lynn M. Zott, book editors.
    p. cm. -- (Opposing viewpoints)
    Summary: "Medical Marijuana: Opposing Viewpoints is the leading source for libraries and classrooms in need of current-issue materials. The viewpoints are selected from a wide range of highly respected sources and publications"-- Provided by publisher.
    Includes bibliographical references and index.
    ISBN 978-0-7377-6056-9 (hardback) -- ISBN 978-0-7377-6057-6 (paperback)
    1. Marijuana--Therapeutic use--United States. 2. Marijuana--Law and legislation--United States. I. Haerens, Margaret. II. Zott, Lynn M. (Lynn Marie), 1969-
    RM666.C266M432 2012
    615.7'8270973--dc23
                                                                        2012006811

Printed in the United States of America
1 2 3 4 5 6 7 16 15 14 13 12

Contents

Chapter 3: How Should Access to Medical Marijuana Be Managed?

Why Consider Opposing Viewpoints?

"The only way in which a human being can make some approach to knowing the whole of a subject is by hearing what can be said about it by persons of every variety of opinion and studying all modes in which it can be looked at by every character of mind. No wise man ever acquired his wisdom in any mode but this."

John Stuart Mill

In our media-intensive culture it is not difficult to find differing opinions. Thousands of newspapers and magazines and dozens of radio and television talk shows resound with differing points of view. The difficulty lies in deciding which opinion to agree with and which "experts" seem the most credible. The more inundated we become with differing opinions and claims, the more essential it is to hone critical reading and thinking skills to evaluate these ideas. Opposing Viewpoints books address this problem directly by presenting stimulating debates that can be used to enhance and teach these skills. The varied opinions contained in each book examine many different aspects of a single issue. While examining these conveniently edited opposing views, readers can develop critical thinking skills such as the ability to compare and contrast authors' credibility, facts, argumentation styles, use of persuasive techniques, and other stylistic tools. In short, the Opposing Viewpoints Series is an ideal way to attain the higher-level thinking and reading skills so essential in a culture of diverse and contradictory opinions.

In addition to providing a tool for critical thinking, Opposing Viewpoints books challenge readers to question their own strongly held opinions and assumptions. Most people form their opinions on the basis of upbringing, peer pressure, and personal, cultural, or professional bias. By reading carefully balanced opposing views, readers must directly confront new ideas as well as the opinions of those with whom they disagree. This is not to argue simplistically that everyone who reads opposing views will—or should—change his or her opinion. Instead, the series enhances readers' understanding of their own views by encouraging confrontation with opposing ideas. Careful examination of others' views can lead to the readers' understanding of the logical inconsistencies in their own opinions, perspective on why they hold an opinion, and the consideration of the possibility that their opinion requires further evaluation.

Evaluating Other Opinions

To ensure that this type of examination occurs, Opposing Viewpoints books present all types of opinions. Prominent spokespeople on different sides of each issue as well as well-known professionals from many disciplines challenge the reader. An additional goal of the series is to provide a forum for other, less known, or even unpopular viewpoints. The opinion of an ordinary person who has had to make the decision to cut off life support from a terminally ill relative, for example, may be just as valuable and provide just as much insight as a medical ethicist's professional opinion. The editors have two additional purposes in including these less known views. One, the editors encourage readers to respect others' opinions—even when not enhanced by professional credibility. It is only by reading or listening to and objectively evaluating others' ideas that one can determine whether they are worthy of consideration. Two, the inclusion of such viewpoints encourages the important critical thinking skill of objectively evaluating an author's credentials and bias. This evaluation will illuminate an author's reasons for taking a particular stance on an issue and will aid in readers' evaluation of the author's ideas.

It is our hope that these books will give readers a deeper understanding of the issues debated and an appreciation of the complexity of even seemingly simple issues when good and honest people disagree. This awareness is particularly important in a democratic society such as ours in which people enter into public debate to determine the common good. Those with whom one disagrees should not be regarded as enemies but rather as people whose views deserve careful examination and may shed light on one's own.

Thomas Jefferson once said that "difference of opinion leads to inquiry, and inquiry to truth." Jefferson, a broadly educated man, argued that "if a nation expects to be ignorant and free . . . it expects what never was and never will be." As individuals and as a nation, it is imperative that we consider the opinions of others and examine them with skill and discernment. The Opposing Viewpoints Series is intended to help readers achieve this goal.

David L. Bender and Bruno Leone,
Founders

Introduction

"*The Justice Department going after
sick individuals using [marijuana] as a
palliative instead of going after serious
criminals makes no sense.*"

*Barack Obama, July 21, 2007,
Manchester, New Hampshire*

Marijuana has long been appreciated for its medicinal value. The presence of cannabis, a genus of flowering plants also known as marijuana, can be traced back to Asia around the Stone Age. It is thought that cannabis spread throughout Asia in the Neolithic era, as nomadic tribes in the region began to develop agricultural practices. Hemp, a valuable fiber found on the stem of cannabis plants, was used to make textiles, and hemp seeds were ground into powder for food and tea. It is believed that early people also used cannabis for medicinal and recreational purposes.

The earliest evidence of the widespread use of hemp can be dated to the Yangshao, a Neolithic society in China situated along the Yellow River around 6,500 years ago. Archeologists have found that hemp was used in clothing, nets for fishing, and rope. During this time, people also put sacrificial vessels filled with hemp seed and other grains inside tombs.

There is evidence that people realized the medicinal effects of cannabis around that time. The oldest pharmacopeia in the world, the Pen Ts'ao Ching, can be dated back to the reign of legendary Chinese emperor Shen Nung around the year 2737 BC. The ancient pharmaceutical guide recommends the use of marijuana to treat conditions such as gout, rheumatism, malaria, menstrual pain, childbirth, and poor memory. The book also notes that ingesting too much of the flowering top of cannabis plants will produce wild hallucinations, or "seeing devils."

As trade expanded from China to other civilizations, cannabis spread throughout India, Asia, Mongolia, the Middle East, and North Africa. Chinese inventions, especially cannabis oil and hemp paper, were immensely popular in other cultures and established hemp as one of the most important and versatile crops in the ancient world.

In India, marijuana became a cornerstone in rituals for certain Hindu sects. The drug was considered sacred and was recommended for the relief of stress and anxiety. Tribes in Africa also smoked marijuana for spiritual and medicinal reasons. In other cultures, cannabis was grown for hemp, which was a valuable and popular fiber for centuries. Archeologists have traced the first-known evidence of hemp in Europe to campsites in Germany and other countries. Hemp was essential in sea-faring countries, where it was used extensively in ropes, nets, and ship riggings.

It was early settlers who brought the cannabis plant to the United States, where hemp was widely cultivated and utilized for a number of products and uses. During the 1700s subsidies were offered to settlers to encourage hemp cultivation and the manufacture of rope and canvas.

In the mid-1800s, the medicinal value of cannabis was popularized through the work of an enterprising Irish physician, William O'Shaughnessy, who discovered the drug's therapeutic properties while working in India for the British East India Company. His successful treatment of rheumatism as well as symptoms of rabies, cholera, and tetanus with marijuana resin was groundbreaking in Western medicine. Before long, physicians in the United Kingdom and the United States were prescribing marijuana for a range of conditions, including incontinence, venereal disease, and skin rashes.

By the late nineteenth century, however, cotton had largely replaced hemp as a major cash crop in the United States. Instead of growing hemp, manufacturers relied on other fibers or imported hemp from other countries. Marijuana was still being utilized for its medicinal qualities; it was listed in the United States Pharmacopeia from 1850 to 1941. In the early twentieth century, the recreational aspect of marijuana caught on with musicians, artists, and people in show business. Alarmed by the rising popularity of marijuana use, the US Federal Bureau of Narcotics initiated a campaign to depict marijuana as a dangerous, addictive substance that would lure young people into a life of drug addiction. The campaign worked. By 1937, twenty-three states had outlawed marijuana. That same year, the US government passed the Marihuana Tax Act, which made it illegal to use marijuana except for medical purposes.

Medical marijuana was finally outlawed by the federal government with the passage of the Controlled Substances Act of 1970. The law declared that marijuana had no proven and accepted medicinal use and classified it as a Schedule I drug, along with addictive and dangerous substances such as heroin and LSD. The US government also tightened its grip on scientific research that focused on the medicinal potential of marijuana to treat disease.

As recently as 2011, the federal government has rebuffed requests to reclassify marijuana as a less dangerous and addictive drug. Instead, marijuana remains classified as a highly addictive drug with no known medicinal use. However, many scientists and researchers argue that marijuana can successfully treat conditions such as chronic pain and nausea, anxiety, post-traumatic stress disorder, and glaucoma. A number of states have passed medical marijuana laws that contravene the federal government's policies on medical marijuana. Further, public opinion has shifted dramatically toward legalization of marijuana, especially for medicinal use.

Opposing Viewpoints: Medical Marijuana explores the issue of medical marijuana in the following chapters: Should Medical Marijuana Be Legal?, Is Medical Marijuana Good for Society?,

How Should Access to Medical Marijuana Be Managed?, and What Are Legal Issues for Patients Who Use Medical Marijuana? The authors in this volume provide insight into emerging legal issues surrounding medical marijuana, debate access to the drug, and consider whether legalizing medical marijuana is medically and socially beneficial for the United States.

CHAPTER 1

Should Medical Marijuana Be Legal?

Chapter Preface

The US federal government's stance on medical marijuana stems from the passage of the Comprehensive Drug Abuse Prevention and Control Act of 1970. It is this key piece of legislation that created the five schedules, or classifications, that remain at the heart of the ongoing controversy over the federal government's treatment of medical marijuana.

By 1969 President Richard Nixon was looking for a way to consolidate existing federal drug control laws into one powerful federal statute to better combat what many felt was a growing problem: the proliferation of drugs—especially dangerous and addictive ones like heroin and cocaine—across the United States. Crime and violence associated with drugs were also major problems in many areas. Nixon began to refer to the effort as a "war," a term that would later be amplified by successive presidential administrations.

Nixon turned to his attorney general, John Mitchell, to craft a piece of legislation that would not only consolidate the federal drug laws, but expand police power and broaden the scope of the government's drug laws. In 1970 they introduced the Comprehensive Drug Abuse Prevention and Control Act. Congress passed it, and the law went into effect on May 1, 1971. As the US Drug Enforcement Administration (DEA) outlines the law's accomplishments: "This law, along with its implementing regulations, established a single system of control for both narcotic and psychotropic drugs for the first time in US history. It also established five schedules that classify controlled substances according to how dangerous they are, their potential for abuse and addiction, and whether they possess legitimate medical value." These five schedules would generate a bit of controversy over the years.

According to the Controlled Substances Act (CSA), which falls under the Comprehensive Drug Abuse Prevention and Control

Act, Schedule I controlled substances are the most addictive and have the highest danger of abuse. They also hold no accepted medical value; therefore, no prescriptions should be written for Schedule I substances. Drugs classified as Schedule I substances include marijuana, heroin, GHB (Gamma-Hydroxybutyric acid), ecstasy, peyote, and LSD (lysergic acid diethylamide; also known as "acid").

Schedule II substances are defined as drugs that are addictive and have high potential for abuse, but have a known and accepted medical value under certain restrictions. Included in this category are cocaine, methadone, opium, morphine, oxycodone, Adderall, and secobarbital. Schedule III substances carry a lower risk for addiction and also have an accepted medicinal use. Schedule IV and V drugs have a decreasing danger of abuse and addiction and have known medicinal value.

Over the years there has been heated controversy over the classification of marijuana as a Schedule I substance. Many medical experts believe that it should not be in the same category as heroin and LSD. Others argue that marijuana is not as addictive as Schedule II drugs such as morphine, opium, and cocaine. With many scientists and researchers asserting the medicinal value of marijuana to treat conditions such as chronic pain and nausea, anxiety, post-traumatic stress disorder, and glaucoma, many medical marijuana supporters believe that the government's refusal to reclassify cannabis (from Schedule I to Schedule II) is based on politics, not scientific and medical research.

The controversy over reclassifying cannabis is one of the subjects explored in the following chapter, which debates the question of whether medical marijuana should be a legal drug. Authors also examine whether medical marijuana will lead to full legalization of marijuana in the United States.

> *"If these patients truly find comfort by using medical marijuana, the federal government should not deliberately deny prolonged pain relieving treatments."*

Medical Marijuana Should Be Legal

Daniel J. Pfeifer

Daniel J. Pfeifer is a law student and contributor to the Touro Law Review. *In the following viewpoint, he argues that federal laws to prohibit the use of medicinal marijuana violate the autonomy of physicians and patients. Pfeifer maintains that the federal government should not stand in the way of patients who use marijuana to alleviate pain and suffering from a number of medical conditions. The best option, he argues, is to reclassify marijuana as a less dangerous and addictive drug so that it will be available for further independent research.*

As you read, consider the following questions:

1. What states does the author say are considering medical marijuana laws as of 2011?

Daniel J. Pfeifer, "Smoking Gun: The Moral and Legal Struggle for Medical Marijuana Social Perspectives," *Touro Law Review*, vol. 7, no. 2, October 11, 2011, pp. 339–41, 249–54, 375–77. Copyright © 2011 by the Touro Law Review. All rights reserved. Reproduced by permission.

2. According to the author, what is the earliest account of marijuana being used for medicinal purposes?
3. How does the author describe marijuana's effect on nausea and vomiting?

In the debate over medical marijuana, the primary justification advanced by its supporters is that marijuana use, especially by terminally ill patients, mitigates their "suffering from [unnecessary] chronic and unbearable pain that persists until death." Currently, Washington D.C. and fourteen states have approved and finalized medical marijuana statutes: Alaska, California, Colorado, Hawaii, Maine, Michigan, Montana, Nevada, New Jersey, New Mexico, Oregon, Rhode Island, Vermont, and Washington. Maryland and Arizona have approved legislation favorable to the use of medical marijuana, but have not legalized its use. Additionally, "New York, Illinois, Delaware, South Dakota . . . and Kansas" are in the process of considering medical marijuana laws.

Although all patients should have the right to treatment, rights, generally, must be considered within the context of national policy. Currently, the federal government has remained hesitant to support detailed medical research and advocacy for medical marijuana. Under the Uniform Controlled Substances Act, marijuana remains a Schedule I drug, meaning possession of it is still illegal and may only be utilized for research purposes. As "the sole Federal agency that approves drug products as safe and effective for intended" purposes, the Federal Drug Administration ("FDA") firmly maintains that marijuana has no medicinal value. Consequently, the federal government has been in continuous conflict with states that have legalized medical marijuana.

According to the American Medical Association, when a physician believes a law is unjust, he or she should work to change the law. If medical marijuana is one treatment a physician can prescribe to alleviate a patient's pain and suffering, then the physician must promote the best interests of the patient by maintaining his or her well being and health. Ultimately, the federal government's prohibition on access to and use of medical marijuana to alleviate pain in terminally ill patients infringes upon their autonomy, which includes their rights to live and avoid severe physical suffering, the right to receive medical treatment, and the right to die with the dignity that comes from one's own choices. If these patients truly find comfort by using medical marijuana, the federal government should not deliberately deny prolonged pain relieving treatments that improve a terminally ill patient's quality of life. . . .

Marijuana as Medicine: Fact or Illusion?

Marijuana has been used medicinally for over five thousand years, with the earliest accounts dating back to China in the third millennium, B.C., where it was used to treat malaria and rheumatic pain. "In India, marijuana [was] used in Ayurvedic medicine," as early as the Tenth Century, to treat various ailments, including "diarrhea, diabetes, tuberculosis, asthma, elephantiasis, anemia, and rabies." In the Middle East, marijuana's medicinal value was recognized as early as the Seventh Century, B.C., and "during . . . the Roman Empire, marijuana was used as an analgesic and anesthetic." In Europe, marijuana was recommended as medicine around 65 A.D. and was used well into the Nineteenth Century. In the United States, physicians recognized marijuana's medicinal value as early as 1850 by listing it in the United States Pharmacopoeia "as a treatment for . . . neuralgia, tetanus, typhus, . . . leprosy, . . . gout, . . . insanity, . . . among others."

Originating from the leaves of the hemp plant, *Cannabis Sativa*, or marijuana, contains over 460 known compounds of which sixty are unique to marijuana, and are commonly referred to as cannabinoids. "Delta-9-tetrahydrocannabinol [("THC")], one of the most psychoactive ingredients in marijuana," eliminates "[l]oss of appetite, nausea, and vomiting" in cancer patients undergoing chemotherapy. Moreover, while THC may increase feelings of depression, these symptoms depend largely on the dose, as well as the psychological and physiological makeup of the patient. Most importantly, THC serves as an analgesic that decreases sensitivity to pain.

Medicinal Value

Through a study conducted by the National Institutes of Health ("NIH") in February 1997, five areas in which medical marijuana may provide therapeutic value were identified, though further research is still required.

Wasting Syndrome: AIDS and Cancer

Many patients with AIDS (acquired immunodeficiency syndrome) or cancer are affected with significant weight loss and decreased caloric intake. "Symptoms of AIDS wasting syndrome include an involuntary weight loss of at least ten percent with chronic diarrhea, weakness, or fever for thirty days or more. . . ." In order to achieve weight gain, some of these patients have smoked medical marijuana to stimulate their appetite and food intake. Additionally, "inhaled marijuana increases appetite and food intake in healthy persons." Since "there are no current cost-effective treatments for the wasting of AIDS or cancer," medical marijuana may be an appropriate treatment upon further research to determine its safety and effectiveness.

Nausea and Vomiting

For many cancer patients undergoing chemotherapy, the various treatments and drugs, such as pharmacologic agents (5-HT3 receptor antagonists), often produce side effects of emesis (vomiting and nausea). Although antiemetic drugs are often prescribed to cancer patients, these medications often fail to work once emesis develops. Since early treatment is the only way to truly deter emesis, many cancer patients inevitably suffer from such intense side effects that they forego treatment all together. Searching for an alternative treatment, many cancer patients have smoked medical marijuana to deter emesis. Research shows that "THC reduces the number of retching and vomiting episodes, the degree and duration of nausea, and the volume of emesis in cancer patients undergoing chemotherapy."

Glaucoma

"Glaucoma is a group of diseases that can damage the eye's optic nerve and result in vision loss and blindness." "Glaucoma occurs when the normal fluid pressure inside the eyes slowly rises," wherein intraocular pressure causes intolerable levels of discomfort. Although patients can protect their eyes against serious vision loss with early treatment, many glaucoma patients have resorted to smoking medical marijuana in order to relieve the pressure on their eyes. Although marijuana only provides temporary relief for short durations, marijuana effectively reduces "intraocular pressure, pupil constriction, and conjunctival hyperemia."

Pain and Suffering

Scientists have discovered two cannabinoid receptors, properly identified as CB1 and CB2, that "are present widely in the brain" as part of the human body's natural pain control system. Consequently, marijuana performs a therapeutic function that has enabled cancer patients and patients in general to relieve pain, even if temporarily. Since many current analgesics are only marginally effective, cannabinoids may become a superior treatment in pain therapy, but only after further research is conducted.

Neurologic and Movement Disorders

Lastly, the NIH has found evidence of marijuana relieving neurologic and movement disorders. As an unpredictable disease with no known cause, "[m]ultiple sclerosis [("MS")] affects the central nervous system by damaging nerve fibers," which often results in muscle spasticity where the muscles become "stiff, inflexible, and prone to spasms and cramping." While "[m]ost MS patients experience muscle weakness in their extremities and difficulty with coordination and balance[,]" some patients experience symptoms "severe enough to impair walking or even standing." "MS can [even] produce partial or complete paralysis." Since no cure or effective medication for MS exists, initial research has revealed that smoking marijuana has relieved "spasticity and nocturnal spasms [associated with] multiple sclerosis and partial spinal cord injury."

Furthermore, the Institute of Medicine ("IOM"), in a March 1999 study, concluded that marijuana's benefits are limited to symptom relief, such as pain relief, appetite stimulation for AIDS wasting syndrome, and control of chemotherapy related nausea and vomiting. Despite popular belief, the IOM reported that marijuana was only marginally useful in relieving eye pressure from glaucoma because the effects were only "short-term, and did not outweigh the long-term risks." Moreover, the report reaffirmed that marijuana effectively treated "muscle spasms associated with multiple sclerosis." However, despite these findings, "the IOM advised that marijuana [should] be considered . . . only when patients [did not receive] enough relief from currently available drugs." While the IOM cautioned "that 'the benefits of smoking marijuana were limited by the toxic effects of the smoke, [the study] nonetheless recommended'" that patients be permitted to smoke marijuana when other therapies failed "on a short-term basis under close supervision." . . .

A Patient's Rights

In the pursuit of autonomy, the patient and physician's primary focus is to protect the patient's independent process of self-definition. Regardless of the identity that a terminally ill patient seeks to adopt or keep, autonomy requires an individual to be free from constraints including death, pain and suffering, and indignity at the end of life. As President Obama's administration continues to impact American culture, patients may finally gain the support they need to access legal medical marijuana. Through the collaborative efforts of President Obama and Attorney General Eric Holder, the U.S. Department of Justice will seek criminal charges against medical marijuana users only when both state and federal laws have been violated. Additionally, medical marijuana clinics will be free of federal investigations provided their operations are lawful.

As autonomous persons, patients have the right to make decisions regarding their bodies and to seek any and all medical treatment to alleviate pain and suffering and preserve life. This right entitles a patient to non-interference from people who might attempt to infringe upon these rights and freedom of choice. Ultimately, a patient should be free to make medical decisions concerning treatment and medication that directly impacts his or her own body. In making decisions concerning a patient's health and well being, patients should be given the right to access medical marijuana for therapeutic purposes. By refusing to allow medical marijuana as an alternative pain treatment, the federal government has infringed upon a patient's fundamental right of autonomy.

While the federal government should not persecute patients using medical marijuana for treatment, medical marijuana should be carefully regulated and patients should be given access to medical marijuana in controlled doses under controlled conditions. Like any medication, marijuana presents its own set of benefits and risks. While smoking marijuana may not be the safest method to deliver THC through the body, other methods such as ingesting oral forms of synthetically government approved THC, for example Marinol, have their own drawbacks. Just like tobacco, smoking marijuana may require the use of filters to reduce the amount of harmful chemicals entering the body. Although marijuana should not necessarily be legalized across the board, it should be at least removed from Schedule I to Schedule II. However, the medical marijuana debate will only be resolved through further government funded, independent research.

> "Smoked marijuana has not withstood the rigors of science—it is not medicine, and it is not safe."

Medical Marijuana Should Not Be Legal

US Department of Justice Drug Enforcement Administration

The US Drug Enforcement Administration (DEA) is a federal government agency tasked with enforcing drug laws and fighting the problem of drug smuggling. In the following viewpoint, the DEA states that marijuana, particularly when it is smoked, has not been conclusively proven to have medicinal value. In fact, the DEA asserts, it has a high potential for abuse and can be dangerous in many circumstances. Therefore, the DEA concludes marijuana is properly classified as a Schedule I controlled substance and should not be reclassified and legalized for medicinal purposes.

As you read, consider the following questions:

1. How many states have approved the use of medical marijuana as of January 2011, according to the viewpoint?

US Department of Justice Drug Enforcement Administration, "The Fallacy of Marijuana for Medicinal Use," *The DEA Position on Marijuana*, January 2011.

2. What method of delivery does the American Society of Addiction Medicine support when it comes to medical marijuana?

3. According to the DEA, how many researchers are registered with the DEA to perform studies with marijuana and its derivatives?

Marijuana is properly categorized under Schedule I of the Controlled Substances Act (CSA). 21 U.S.C. § 801, et seq. The clear weight of the currently available evidence supports this classification, including evidence that smoked marijuana has a high potential for abuse, has no accepted medicinal value in treatment in the United States, and evidence that there is a general lack of accepted safety for its use even under medical supervision.

Misconceptions About Marijuana

The campaign to legitimize what is called "medical" marijuana is based on two propositions: first, that science views marijuana as medicine; and second, that the DEA targets sick and dying people using the drug. Neither proposition is true. Specifically, smoked marijuana has not withstood the rigors of science—it is not medicine, and it is not safe. Moreover, the DEA targets criminals engaged in the cultivation and trafficking of marijuana, not the sick and dying. This is true even in the 15 states that have approved the use of "medical" marijuana.

On October 19, 2009 Attorney General Eric Holder announced formal guidelines for federal prosecutors in states that have enacted laws authorizing the use of marijuana for medical purposes. The guidelines, as set forth in a memorandum from Deputy Attorney General David W. Ogden, make clear that the focus of federal resources should not be on individuals whose actions are in compliance with existing state laws, and underscores that the Department will continue to prosecute people whose claims of compliance with state and local law conceal operations inconsistent with the terms, conditions, or purposes of the law. He also reiterated that the Department of Justice is committed to the enforcement of the Controlled Substances Act in all states and that this guidance does not "legalize" marijuana or provide for legal defense to a violation of federal law. While some people have interpreted these guidelines to mean that the federal government has relaxed its policy on "medical" marijuana, this in fact is not the case. Investigations and prosecutions of violations of state and federal law will continue. These are the guidelines DEA has and will continue to follow.

Smoked Marijuana Is Not Medicine

In 1970, Congress enacted laws against marijuana based in part on its conclusion that marijuana has no scientifically proven medical value. Likewise, the Food and Drug Administration (FDA), which is responsible for approving drugs as safe and effective medicine, has thus far declined to approve smoked marijuana for any condition or disease. Indeed, the FDA has noted that "there is currently sound evidence that smoked marijuana is harmful," and "that no sound scientific studies support medical use of marijuana for treatment in the United States, and no animal or human data support the safety or efficacy of marijuana for general medical use."

The United States Supreme Court has also declined to carve out an exception for marijuana under a theory of medical viability. In 2001, for example, the Supreme Court decided that a 'medical necessity' defense against prosecution was unavailable to defendants because Congress had purposely placed marijuana into Schedule I, which enumerates those controlled substances without any medical benefits [*United States v. Oakland Cannabis Buyers' Cooperative et al.* (2001)].

Gonzales v. Raich

In *Gonzales v. Raich*, 545 U.S. 1 (2005), the Court had another opportunity to create a type of 'medical necessity' defense in a case involving severely ill California residents who had received physician approval to cultivate and use marijuana under California's Compassionate Use Act (CUA). . . . Despite the state's attempt to shield its residents from liability under CUA, the Supreme Court held that Congress' power to regulate interstate drug markets included the authority to regulate wholly intrastate markets as well. Consequently, the Court again declined to carve out a 'medical necessity' defense, finding that the CSA was not diminished in the face of any state law to the contrary and could support the specific enforcement actions at issue.

In a show of support for the *Raich* decision, the International Narcotics Control Board (INCB) issued this statement urging other countries to consider the real dangers of cannabis:

> Cannabis is classified under international conventions as a drug with a number of personal and public health problems. It is not a 'soft' drug as some people would have you believe. There is new evidence confirming well-known mental health problems, and some countries with a more liberal policy towards cannabis are reviewing their position. Countries need to take a strong stance towards cannabis abuse.

The DEA and the federal government are not alone in viewing smoked marijuana as having no documented medical value. Voices in the medical community likewise do not accept smoked marijuana as medicine:

- The American Medical Association (AMA) has always endorsed "well-controlled studies of marijuana and related cannabinoids in patients with serious conditions for which preclinical, anecdotal, or controlled evidence suggests possible efficacy and the application of such results to the understanding and treatment of disease." In November 2009, the AMA amended its policy, urging that marijuana's status as a Schedule I controlled substance be reviewed "with the goal of facilitating the conduct of clinical research and development of cannabinoid-based medicines, and alternate delivery methods." The AMA also stated that "this should not be viewed as an endorsement of state-based medical cannabis programs, the legalization of marijuana, or that scientific evidence on the therapeutic use of cannabis meets the current standards for prescription drug product."

- The American Society of Addiction Medicine's (ASAM) public policy statement on "Medical Marijuana," clearly rejects smoking as a means of drug delivery. ASAM further recommends that "all cannabis, cannabis-based products and cannabis delivery devices should be subject to the same standards applicable to all other prescription medication and medical devices, and should not be distributed or otherwise provided to patients . . ." without FDA approval. ASAM also "discourages state interference in the federal medication approval process."

- The American Cancer Society (ACS) "does not advocate inhaling smoke, nor the legalization of marijuana," although the organization does support carefully controlled clinical studies for alternative delivery methods, specifically a tetrahydrocannabinol (THC) skin patch.

- The American Glaucoma Society (AGS) has stated that "although marijuana can lower the intraocular pressure, the side effects and short duration of action, coupled with the lack of evidence that its use alters the course of glaucoma, preclude recommending this drug in any form for the treatment of glaucoma at the present time."

- The American Academy of Pediatrics (AAP) believes that "[a]ny change in the legal status of marijuana, even if limited to adults, could affect the prevalence of use among adolescents." While it supports scientific research on the possible medical use of cannabinoids as opposed to smoked marijuana, it opposes the legalization of marijuana.

16 States and DC That Have Enacted Laws to Legalize Medical Marijuana

State	Year Passed
1. Alaska	1998
2. Arizona	2010
3. California	1996
4. Colorado	2000
5. DC	2010
6. Delaware	2011
7. Hawaii	2000
8. Maine	1999
9. Michigan	2008
10. Montana	2004
11. Nevada	2000
12. New Jersey	2010
13. New Mexico	2007
14. Oregon	1998
15. Rhode Island	2006
16. Vermont	2004
17. Washington	1998

TAKEN FROM: Medical Marijuana. procon.org, 2011.

- The National Multiple Sclerosis Society (NMSS) has stated that it could not recommend medical marijuana be made widely available for people with multiple sclerosis for symptom management, explaining: "This decision was not only based on existing legal barriers to its use but, even more importantly, because studies to date do not demonstrate a clear benefit compared to existing symptomatic therapies and because side effects, systemic effects, and long-term effects are not yet clear."

• The British Medical Association (BMA) voiced extreme concern that downgrading the criminal status of marijuana would "mislead" the public into believing that the drug is safe. The BMA maintains that marijuana "has been linked to greater risk of heart disease, lung cancer, bronchitis and emphysema." The 2004 Deputy Chairman of the BMA's Board of Science said that "[t]he public must be made aware of the harmful effects we know result from smoking this drug."

The Institute of Medicine Study

In 1999, the Institute of Medicine (IOM) released a landmark study reviewing the supposed medical properties of marijuana. The study is frequently cited by "medical" marijuana advocates, but in fact severely undermines their arguments.

• After release of the IOM study, the principal investigators cautioned that the active compounds in marijuana may have medicinal potential and therefore should be researched further. However, the study concluded that "there is little future in smoked marijuana as a medically approved medication."

• For some ailments, the IOM found ". . . potential therapeutic value of cannabinoid drugs, primarily THC, for pain relief, control of nausea and vomiting, and appetite stimulation." However, it pointed out that "[t]he effects of cannabinoids on the symptoms studied are generally modest, and in most cases there are more effective medications [than smoked marijuana]."

• The study concluded that, at best, there is only anecdotal information on the medical benefits of smoked marijuana for some ailments, such as muscle spasticity. For other ailments, such as epilepsy and glaucoma, the study found no evidence of medical value and did not endorse further research.

- The IOM study explained that "smoked marijuana . . . is a crude THC delivery system that also delivers harmful substances." In addition, "plants contain a variable mixture of biologically active compounds and cannot be expected to provide a precisely defined drug effect." Therefore, the study concluded that "there is little future in smoked marijuana as a medically approved medication."

- The principal investigators explicitly stated that using smoked marijuana in clinical trials "should not be designed to develop it as a licensed drug, but should be a stepping stone to the development of new, safe delivery systems of cannabinoids."

Thus, even scientists and researchers who believe that certain active ingredients in marijuana may have potential medicinal value openly *discount the notion that smoked marijuana is or can become "medicine."*

DEA Studies on Medical Marijuana

The Drug Enforcement Administration supports ongoing research into potential medicinal uses of marijuana's active ingredients. As of December 2010:

- There are 111 researchers registered with DEA to perform studies with marijuana, marijuana extracts, and non-tetrahydrocannabinol marijuana derivatives that exist in the plant, such as cannabidiol and cannabinol.

- Studies include evaluation of abuse potential, physical/psychological effects, adverse effects, therapeutic potential, and detection.

- Fourteen of the researchers are approved to conduct research with smoked marijuana on human subjects.

At present, however, *the clear weight of the evidence is that smoked marijuana is harmful.* No matter what medical condition has been studied, other drugs already approved by the FDA have been proven to be safer than smoked marijuana.

The only drug currently approved by the FDA that contains the synthetic form of THC is Marinol®. Available through prescription, Marinol® comes in pill form, and is used to relieve nausea and vomiting associated with chemotherapy for cancer patients and to assist with loss of appetite with AIDS patients.

Sativex®, an oromucosal spray for the treatment of spasticity due to Multiple Sclerosis is already approved for use in Canada and was approved in June 2010 for use in the United Kingdom. The oral liquid spray contains two of the cannabinoids found in marijuana—THC and cannabidiol (CBD)—but unlike smoked marijuana, removes contaminants, reduces the intoxicating effects, is grown in a structured and scientific environment, administers a set dosage and meets criteria for pharmaceutical products.

Organizers behind the "medical" marijuana movement have not dealt with ensuring that the product meets the standards of modern medicine: quality, safety and efficacy. There is no standardized composition or dosage; no appropriate prescribing information; no quality control; no accountability for the product; no safety regulation; no way to measure its effectiveness (besides anecdotal stories); and no insurance coverage. Science, not popular vote, should determine what medicine is.

"Rescheduling medical cannabis is the
first step in developing a comprehensive
federal policy."

The US Government Should Reclassify Marijuana as a Medically Acceptable Drug

Americans for Safe Access

Americans for Safe Access (ASA) is an organization that promotes the use of medical marijuana. In the following viewpoint, the ASA evaluates the Barack Obama administration's policy on medical marijuana. The group concludes that the federal government has worked to circumvent state laws on medical marijuana and has stepped a strategy of intimidation and criminal enforcement raids on legal medical marijuana dispensaries. There is, the group declares, also widespread discrimination in housing and employment against people who have legal prescriptions to use medical marijuana. The ASA maintains that one of the key solutions to this impasse between state and federal governments is for the Drug Enforcement Administration (DEA) to reclassify cannabis as a medically acceptable drug.

As you read, consider the following questions:

1. According to the ASA, President Obama is responsible for how many aggressive criminal enforcement raids in medical cannabis states since taking office in January 2009?

2. What states have enacted explicit protections from discrimination on housing and jobs for people who use medical marijuana, according to the viewpoint?

3. How does the ASA say that the DEA has responded to a petition filed in 2002 about rescheduling marijuana as a less dangerous drug?

While the prevailing public perception is that President Obama has addressed the issue of medical cannabis, that perception could not be further from the truth. During his campaign, then-Senator Obama told the *Medford Mail Tribune* regarding medical cannabis, "I'm not going to be using Justice Department resources to try to circumvent state laws on this issue." After several members of the Obama Administration stated publicly that the federal government would not interfere with state medical cannabis laws, the Justice Department issued a memo in October 2009 putting that new policy into writing. Advocates hailed this apparent policy change as a victory for patients across the country.

Eighteen months later, we've had a chance to assess the Obama Administration's track record, with respect to not just federal enforcement, but also civil rights—such as protections from housing and employment discrimination, the ability of veterans to access medical marijuana, and the impact that federal regulators and taxation have on local distribution centers.

Americans for Safe Access gives the Obama Administration an "F" for failing to address medical cannabis as a public health issue.

Enforcement—Grade F

Even if President Obama was keeping his word about not "using Justice Department resources to try to circumvent state laws," it would still be insufficient to address medical cannabis as a national public health issue. Unfortunately, President Obama has not been able to adhere to either the spirit or the letter of his new policy.

Raids and Intimidation

President Obama is responsible for new intimidation strategies and more than 100 aggressive criminal enforcement raids in medical cannabis states since taking office in January 2009. By comparison, former President George W. Bush conducted just over 200 such raids during his eight years in office. Since the Justice Department memo was issued in October 2009, the Obama Administration has used federal agencies to execute at least 87 raids, resulting in no fewer than 27 indictments. President Obama, with the help of DEA Administrator Michele Leonhart, a Bush-holdover, is set to surpass his predecessor's abysmal record on medical cannabis raids, despite his new policy and enforcement promises.

- In just two months, March and April 2011, there were 35 federal raids in four states. Not since the height of federal enforcement in 2007 have there been so many raids in such a short period of time.

- On the day the Montana State Senate was to vote on a bill repealing the voter-approved medical cannabis law, the federal government executed 26 search warrants in that state and made arrests.

- In April 2011, U.S. Attorneys in the Obama Justice Department sent a letter to Washington's governor threatening state officials with criminal prosecution if they implement a distribution licensing system designed by the legislature.

• In 2010, the DEA went to federal court in Michigan to
obtain confidential medical records for qualified patients,
despite state law making their release a crime. In March
2011, the DEA raided a Michigan physician's office seizing
more than 3,000 private patient records.

If any pattern has emerged, it is that the federal government
has targeted vulnerable communities in an effort to undermine
local and state laws.

Prosecutions

Dozens of federal medical cannabis defendants are still being
prosecuted as a result of the aggressive enforcement policies of
Pres. G.W. Bush. Rather than sending these cases to state court
where they should be tried, the Obama Administration has continued to vigorously prosecute them in federal court, despite
concerns raised by several federal judges. In fact, federal prosecutors continue to recommend harsh punitive sentences, which
in some cases have been rejected by federal judges. For example,
Charles Lynch was sentenced to one year and one day and James
Stacey was sentenced to probation only, though both were subject to lengthy minimum sentences.

The continuing prosecution of Bush-era cases is bad enough,
but the Justice Department has chosen to prosecute more than
two-dozen newly indicted patients, providers, and caregivers.

A few examples include:

• Chris Bartkowicz, a licensed grower whose Colorado
home was raided by the Drug Enforcement
Administration the day after he was interviewed by a local
news station, was sentenced to five years in prison.

• Kristen Krusyna was arrested with 14 others in Nevada
for providing access to the sick patients of Las Vegas. She
currently faces prosecution for possession with intent to
distribute under the federal Controlled Substances Act.

- Two qualified California patients, Dr. Mollie Fry and her husband, attorney Dale Schafer, were convicted and each sentenced to five years in prison. Although Fry and Schafer were tried and sentenced during the Bush era, the appeal of their sentence was strenuously opposed by Obama's Justice Department.

Housing and Employment—Grade C–

Despite a recent HUD decision to have local housing authorities address the issue of medical cannabis use and cultivation in public housing, hundreds of thousands of patients across the country are vulnerable to eviction and harassment. For years the federal government's draconian rules on drug use in public housing have been applied to medical cannabis patients.

Patients are equally, if not more, vulnerable to discrimination at the workplace. Court decisions have upheld such discrimination and, as a result, patients face an uphill battle to achieve rights afforded most others in society. Arizona, Maine, Michigan and Rhode Island have established explicit protections from discrimination on housing and jobs, but such helpful measures are insufficient to address a problem that needs federal leadership. According to a statement by HUD, it is the responsibility of local Housing Authorities to "determine, on a case by case basis, the appropriateness of program termination for the use of medical marijuana." Patients are thus unable to determine whether or not they may use their medication until after they are facing termination.

A few examples include:

- Robert Jones, a New Mexico patient, was told by the Housing Authority that he would be allowed to cultivate and use his medicine, only to later be evicted. Now he is homeless and forever banned from receiving federal housing aid.

- Marcy Doe, a California cancer patient, was forced to choose between complying with a new mandatory drug testing program or lose her job. Rather than forfeit her

job and insurance, she agreed to testing and stopped using cannabis, leaving her to suffer from the severe nausea
caused by chemotherapy.

• James Doe, a Colorado patient, was given a difficult choice
by his landlord, HUD: stop storing and using medical
cannabis at home or lose his voucher. James, a wheelchair-
bound patient who was struck at a young age with a degen-
erative muscle disorder, must now take the city bus to his
friend's house in order to use his medication and obtain
relief from the spasms that wrack his body 24 hours a day.

Financial Services—Grade F

Over the past three years, several large banks and financial institutions have, based on federal law, refused to provide services to
medical cannabis businesses that comply with local and state laws.
These companies include CitiCorp, Wells Fargo, Bank of America,
and credit card service providers. This has caused hardship for
medical cannabis providers who rely on financial institutions to
handle cash and credit card transactions safely and efficiently.

In addition, the Internal Revenue Service under the Obama
Administration has begun audits of state-compliant medical cannabis providers, threatening to bankrupt them by denying their
deductions and demanding more taxes. Recently, it was revealed
that the FDIC is putting pressure on banks to investigate and
report medical cannabis businesses and their financial transactions. Yet when 15 Congressional representatives demanded the
Treasury Department stop threatening banks that provide accounts to medical cannabis patients and providers, the Treasury
Department claimed no such pressure had been applied. Banks
still say Treasury is responsible, and patients and providers continue to have their accounts closed.

Veterans—Grade C–

In 2010, the Department of Veteran Affairs responded to pressure by veterans and patient advocates and improved their policy

What Is a Controlled (Scheduled) Drug?

A *controlled (scheduled)* drug is one whose use and distribution is tightly controlled because of its abuse potential or risk. *Controlled* drugs are rated in the order of their abuse risk and placed in *Schedules* by the Federal Drug Enforcement Administration (DEA). The drugs with the highest abuse potential are placed in *Schedule* I, and those with the lowest abuse potential are in *Schedule* V. These schedules are commonly shown as C-I, C-II, C-III, C-IV, and C-V.

- *Schedule I*—drugs with a high abuse risk. These drugs have NO safe, accepted medical use in the United States. Some examples are heroin, marijuana, LSD, PCP, and crack cocaine.

- *Schedule II*—drugs with a high abuse risk, but also have safe and accepted medical uses in the United States. These drugs . . . include certain narcotic, stimulant, and depressant drugs. Some examples are morphine, cocaine, oxycodone (Percodan®), methylphenidate (Ritalin®), and dextroamphetamine (Dexedrine®).

- *Schedule III, IV, or V*—drugs with an abuse risk less than Schedule II. These drugs . . . include those containing smaller amounts of certain narcotic and non-narcotic drugs, anti-anxiety drugs, tranquilizers, sedatives, stimulants, and non-narcotic analgesics. Some examples are acetaminophen with codeine (Tylenol® No. 3), paregoric, hydrocodone with acetaminophen (Vicodin®), diazepam (Valium®), alprazolam (Xanax®), propoxyphene (Darvon®), and pentazocine (Talwin®).

Source: "Controlled Drugs," Texas State Board of Pharmacy, 2004. www.tsbp.state.tx.us.

on medical cannabis. Previous VA policy treated medical cannabis use as criminal, often resulting in patients who used medical cannabis being denied treatment by the VA. Now the VA recognizes medical cannabis may help some veterans and lets VA physicians decide if cannabis use would interfere with a patient's other medications. VA physicians are still barred from recommending medical cannabis to their patients, forcing veterans to consult doctors outside of the VA system. VA physicians also still ultimately have the authority to deny pharmaceutical medications to patients who use medical cannabis.

Solutions

The biggest impediment to implementation of state medical cannabis laws, as well as to states passing new laws, is the failure of the federal government to adopt a comprehensive medical cannabis policy. Such a policy would include the reclassification of cannabis—a demand made by advocates, scientists and medical experts alike. A comprehensive policy would also discontinue federal raids and prosecutions, leaving states to enforce their own medical cannabis laws. A proactive approach is needed to protect patients' civil rights, such as establishing the safeguards against housing and employment discrimination other members of society enjoy. Finally, although the medical efficacy of cannabis is well established for a number of health conditions, there remains much to learn about this extraordinarily promising therapeutic substance. The federal government must end its stranglehold on research by streamlining the research approval process and expanding the availability of research-grade cannabis.

Rescheduling

In 2002, the Coalition for Rescheduling Cannabis filed a petition with the Drug Enforcement Administration, demanding that the DEA place cannabis in a less restrictive classification, as cannabis has demonstrated considerable medical value and few physical risks. The coalition of patients and patient advocates has been waiting nearly a decade for a decision. The federal strategy of delay has so far prevented the coalition from legally challenging the government's official position that cannabis is a highly dangerous drug with no medical value. Not only has the coalition received no response, but the DEA has refused to respond to Congressional, administrative and other formal requests for information on the petition's status. Rescheduling medical cannabis is the first step in developing a comprehensive federal policy.

Enforcement

The Obama Administration has made many public promises to scale back enforcement against medical cannabis patients and providers, and yet the raids and prosecutions continue. Even if the Administration carved out an exception for medical cannabis states, that would be an inadequate and shortsighted solution. The only way to ensure proper protection for patients and their providers is by developing a comprehensive federal policy. De-emphasizing federal enforcement as part of a comprehensive federal policy would allow millions of sick and dying patients across this country safe access to the medicine their doctors recommend. Free from fear of arrest and prosecution, medical cannabis providers could better focus on providing patients with the medicine they need, while operating in compliance with local or state laws. In addition, a comprehensive federal policy would support civil enforcement by local and state officials rather than the aggressive and harmful federal tactics currently utilized. Under a comprehensive federal policy, any pending federal cases would be discharged to state courts for adjudication of any local or state law violations.

Research

A robust federal research program would provide the mechanisms necessary to allow for multidisciplinary research focusing on the medical benefits of cannabis. This type of federal research program, as part of a comprehensive federal policy, would cut through the red tape that currently exists during the planning stages of cannabis research by removing the onerous review system that currently obstructs most research in the United States. It would also end a decades-long monopoly on research grade cannabis by granting additional licenses to provide alternate sources of supply for FDA-approved clinical trials. Finally, an ideal research program would provide competitive federal grants, encouraging researchers to enter the field and become experts in cannabinoid science. A research program is imperative to fully unlock the extraordinary promise of cannabis and cannabinoid therapeutics, including new, more effective treatments for some of the most devastating conditions. Patients suffering from cancer, multiple sclerosis, Alzheimer's, diabetes, Huntington's, and a host of other fatal or debilitating diseases deserve access to any medication that may help them live longer, more comfortable lives. Hundreds of peer-reviewed scientific studies indicate cannabis has that potential. We need to know more.

> "The DEA said marijuana . . . has an
> elevated possibility of abuse, does not
> have a 'currently accepted medical use
> in treatment' and is not safe to use
> under doctors' supervision."

The US Government Should Not Reclassify Marijuana as a Medically Acceptable Drug

Tom Strode

Tom Strode is a contributor to the Ethics and Religious Liberty Commission of the Southern Baptist Convention. In the following viewpoint, he reports on the commission's support for the Drug Enforcement Administration (DEA) decision to turn down a petition to reclassify marijuana as a drug with an accepted medical use. Supporters of the decision assert that evidence shows that marijuana is an addictive drug that can be very physically destructive, Strode relates. These supporters strongly agree that marijuana must remain a Schedule I drug under the Controlled Substances Act.

As you read, consider the following questions:

1. According to the petition from the Coalition for Rescheduling Cannabis, what should the DEA reclassify marijuana under?
2. How many states have legalized marijuana for medical purposes as of August 2011, according to the author?
3. According to Americans for Safe Access, how many reports and articles support the medical benefits of marijuana?

The federal government's decision to continue to classify marijuana as a hazardous drug with no accepted medical use was the right ruling for the right reason, said a Southern Baptist public policy specialist.

The Drug Enforcement Administration (DEA) announced it had rejected a request by medical marijuana advocates to re-categorize marijuana as a drug with an accepted medical use. Instead, the DEA said marijuana's inclusion in Schedule I of the federal drug regulation regime would stand because it has an elevated possibility of abuse, does not have a "currently accepted medical use in treatment" and is not safe to use under doctors' supervision.

The action was "welcome news," said Barrett Duke, the Ethics & Religious Liberty Commission's vice president for public policy and research.

The Right Reasons

The DEA not only upheld "the government's long-standing position on marijuana, they upheld it for the right reasons," Duke said. "They are correct to recognize that it is prone to be abused. Marijuana is a dangerous substance. It is addictive and serves as the gateway to much more destructive drug use.

"The DEA is also correct in their observation that there are no scientifically credible studies available to support the claims of those who want the drug legalized," he said. "Instead, there are multiple studies available that demonstrate the connection of marijuana use to respiratory disease, risky behavior, addiction and crime. Until credible scientific studies are conducted and convincingly contradict what we already know about the destructive effects of marijuana, this dangerous drug must remain illegal."

The ruling, which was announced July 8 [2011], came in a June 21 letter from DEA Administrator Michele Leonhart to a petitioner who had sought the change in 2002. The petition from the Coalition for Rescheduling Cannabis called for the DEA to reclassify marijuana under Schedule III, IV or V of the Controlled Substances Act.

Under that federal law, Schedule I—unlike the other four categories—contains drugs that have no accepted medical use. In addition to marijuana, Schedule I drugs also include heroin, LSD and Ecstasy.

The Delayed Decision

The nearly nine years that elapsed after the DEA received the petition included a scientific and medical evaluation, plus scheduling recommendation, by the Department of Health and Human Services (HHS). The DEA followed HHS' recommendation and reasoning.

In May, supporters of the medical use of marijuana filed a suit in the U.S. Court of Appeals for the District of Columbia Circuit seeking to force the Obama administration to act on the petition. After the DEA announced its decision, the advocates challenged the ruling July 21 [2011] in D.C. Circuit Court.

Medical marijuana advocates criticized the DEA decision but expressed hope they could prevail in court.

"Although this superficially looks like a defeat for the medical marijuana community, it simply maintains the status quo," said Joe Elford, chief counsel for Americans for Safe Access (ASA), which challenged the DEA action as a member of the Coalition

Negative Health Effects of Marijuana

Single doses can impair cognitive functioning, learning motivation and motor abilities. Very large doses can cause confusion, restlessness, hallucinations and panic reactions. Possible depression of the immune system, chromosome damage, [and] reduced sperm count in males [can also occur].

Source: "Federal Drug Penalties," The Catholic University of America, 2008.
http://counsel.cua.edu.

for Rescheduling Cannabis. "More importantly, however, we have foiled the government's strategy of delay and we can now go head-to-head on the merits, that marijuana really does have therapeutic value."

The Case for Reclassifying Marijuana

The DEA's ruling runs counter to policy developments in the states. Since 1996, 16 states and the District of Columbia have legalized marijuana for medical purposes.

More than 6,500 reports and articles support the medical benefits of marijuana, according to Americans for Safe Access. The organization says research has shown the use of marijuana has helped reduce pain in patients with HIV and multiple sclerosis and has aided in increased appetite among those with the severe lung disease COPD.

In her letter, however, Leonhart said the "known risks of marijuana use have not been shown to be outweighed by specific benefits in well-controlled clinical trials that scientifically evaluate safety and efficacy."

She also refuted the petitioner's assertion that the chances of dependence on marijuana are less than those of other Schedule I, or even Schedule II, drugs. In documents accompanying her letter, HHS says "long-term, regular use of marijuana can lead to physical dependence and withdrawal following discontinuation as well as psychic addiction or dependence," Leonhart wrote.

Further Study of Marijuana Is Needed

The DEA administrator also said marijuana does not have a "currently accepted medical use" because: "The drug's chemistry is not known and reproducible; there are no adequate safety studies; there are no adequate and well-controlled studies proving efficacy; the drug is not accepted by qualified experts; and the scientific evidence is not widely available."

The HHS document accompanying Leonhart's letter cited the following research results among its reasons for not recommending the removal of marijuana from Schedule I: Evidence exists to show sufficient use can establish a hazard to the health of the user or the safety of others, and heavy use of marijuana by smoking impairs such functions as classroom learning and the operation of motor vehicles.

> *"The problem is, the line between legal and illegal regarding marijuana is fading year by year."*

Medical Marijuana Will Open Door to Full Legalization of Marijuana

Christian Science Monitor

The Christian Science Monitor *is an online daily news source and weekly newspaper. In the following viewpoint, the Christian Science Monitor's editorial board contends that the federal government's lax enforcement of marijuana laws is essentially a tacit approval of the use of marijuana for medicinal purposes. Pro-marijuana advocates, the board asserts, will take this approval and push for the full legalization of marijuana. This, according to the board, would be a travesty considering there are lingering questions over the drug's safety and efficacy. The editorial board urges the US Justice Department to enforce all marijuana regulations and stand firmly against the full legalization of marijuana.*

As you read, consider the following questions:

1. What state was the first to legalize marijuana for medicinal purposes, according to the viewpoint?

2. In what year does the viewpoint state that Los Angeles put a moratorium on new marijuana dispensaries?

3. According to Kevin Sabet, how many people out of ten who use marijuana become dependent at some time?

The federal government has limited resources to fight drugs, and funds should not be wasted on prosecuting users and providers of medical marijuana who comply with state laws, the Obama administration said this week.

While this argument may indeed seem a sensible prioritizing of federal effort and dollars, the White House and the public should realize it comes with a cost.

The Consequences of Federal Policy

That cost is Washington's tacit approval of state-sanctioned medical marijuana, which the drug's proponents will take as a green light to push even harder for their ultimate goal: full legalization of marijuana use and distribution.

Backers would like to see the buying and selling of pot regulated and taxed much like alcohol and tobacco. Their patient and well-funded route to this goal is through the states, with one avenue being state legalization of medical marijuana.

Since 1996, 13 states have allowed such use—in defiance of a federal statute that outlaws marijuana as a controlled substance. Meanwhile, the Food and Drug Administration does not approve of marijuana as safe or effective for any medicinal use, and the drug has never gone through the FDA's rigorous approval process. Yet several more states are considering medical marijuana laws at the urging of pro-pot and patients-rights groups.

The Larger Context

Their stated reason is compassion. They argue that marijuana alleviates suffering for certain illnesses. No one wants to deny compassion for the sick, but Americans need to be aware of the larger context in this debate.

To begin with, state medical marijuana laws have opened the door to distribution beyond those who are ill. California shines glaringly as Exhibit A—just like the green neon signs that advertise so many of its medical marijuana dispensaries.

The Golden State was the first to legalize marijuana for medical purposes and its law is notoriously loose. All it takes to buy pot is a doctor's permission—and some doctors are willing to fill prescriptions on the thinnest of pretenses. With hundreds of marijuana storefronts in Los Angeles, the city put a moratorium on new dispensaries in 2007. A Superior Court judge ruled this week that an extension of the moratorium is invalid, a move that is likely to spur the opening of even more pot shops.

Learning from California's Mistakes

Other states have looked aghast at California's experience. They've tried to fashion stricter laws. For example, the Minnesota legislature this year amended a medical marijuana bill so that it applied only to terminally ill patients.

Yet Republican Gov. Tim Pawlenty wisely vetoed the bill in May. He said he shared law enforcement concerns about expanded drug use. (Consider the problems with controlling wider use of prescribed painkillers, for instance). He also noted the lack of federal regulation.

Marijuana as Medicine

The federal regulation question gets at another fundamental issue—the safe use of marijuana as a medicine.

The FDA is not alone in its refusal to sanctify marijuana for medical purposes. Neither does the American Medical Association approve of it—though it has encouraged its study. Doctors hesitate to approve a medicine that is smoked. And questions linger about dosage, purity, and unpredictability.

Generally, marijuana is not nearly as harmless as its proponents make it out to be. While pot cannot directly kill its user the way that alcohol or, say, an overdose of heroin can, heavy use can lead to dependence. About 1 in 10 people who have ever used marijuana become dependent at some time, according to Kevin Sabet, in the 2006 book, *Pot Politics*. Mr. Sabet, a staunch opponent of legalizing marijuana, is now a policy adviser to the president's drug czar, Gil Kerlikowske.

Heavy use can also lead to serious mental-health problems, especially in young people. Even casual use distorts perception, reduces motor skills, and affects alertness—a hazard in driving and other activities.

These concerns should cause the public to stop and rethink its growing support for legal use of marijuana (44 percent, according to an October Gallup poll, up from 34 percent in 2003).

Holding the Line on Marijuana Policy

Thankfully, the Obama administration does not support the legalization of marijuana. And this week's Justice Department directive, which formalized a decision taken last March, by no means lets dispensaries off the hook. The feds will still go after misuse of state medical marijuana laws—prosecuting, for instance, providers that serve minors, launder money, or illegally possess firearms.

"We will not tolerate drug traffickers who hide behind claims of compliance with state law to mask activities that are clearly illegal," Attorney General Eric Holder said.

All well and good. The problem is, the line between legal and illegal regarding marijuana is fading year by year. The pro-pot groups would rub it out altogether. For the sake of a clear-thinking and healthy America, that must not be allowed to happen.

> "I am sensitive to the pain that individuals endure from disease, but that does not make it appropriate to sanction the medical use of marijuana."

Legalizing Medical Marijuana Is Poor Public Policy

Mary Pat Angelini

Mary Pat Angelini is a member of the New Jersey Assembly. In the following viewpoint, she contends that although she is sympathetic to those suffering from disease, medical marijuana should not be legalized by the states. Angelini points out that there are no conclusive studies that prove the efficacy of marijuana as a medicine. She also argues that legalization would send the wrong message to youth by telling them smoking marijuana under some circumstances is fine, but not others. The government, Angelini insists, should maintain a consistent approach to marijuana.

As you read, consider the following questions:

1. According to a Department of Health and Human Services study, how many Americans over the age of twenty-one have tried marijuana at least once?

2. How many pounds of smokeable materials does the average marijuana plant produce every year, according to Angelini?

3. According to the viewpoint, if patients or caregivers are allowed six marijuana plants for harvesting under the proposed New Jersey law, how many pounds of marijuana will a patient harvest per year?

Marijuana is the most commonly used illegal drug in America. According to a national survey performed by the Department of Health and Human Services, nearly 95 million Americans over the age of 21 have tried marijuana at least once. In addition to this alarming statistic, of the 7.1 million Americans suffering from illegal drug dependence or abuse, 60 percent abuse marijuana. These facts alone show that our country is currently struggling to control this substance and make it very clear that policies must be initiated that will further restrict access to this drug vs. granting permission to obtain the substance.

The Food and Drug Administration (FDA)—which opposes the use of smoked marijuana—is the federal agency that certifies what drugs are safe and those that have a medicinal benefit. While I am a supporter of states' rights, it is critical that scientific research be conducted to determine what the ramifications are as a result of smoking a potentially dangerous substance. In 2006, the FDA declared that marijuana has a high potential for abuse, and that there is a lack of accepted safety for its use, even under medical supervision. The very idea of ingesting a "medicine" by smoking it is counterintuitive.

Ill-Considered Legislation

On Dec. 15 [2008], the New Jersey Senate's Health, Human Services and Senior Citizens Committee favorably reported the "New Jersey Compassionate Use Medical Marijuana Act" by a

6-1 vote, with two abstentions. The proposed bill would permit patients, who are diagnosed by a physician as having a debilitating medical condition, to smoke marijuana either by cultivating up to six plants themselves or having it provided by a state-authorized personal caregiver.

The legislation would also empower the Department of Health and Senior Services to establish alternative treatment centers to produce and dispense marijuana for medical purposes to those possessing a registry identification card. Currently, 13 other states permit the use of marijuana for medical purposes.

The potential for this legislation to become law is ill-advised public policy. I empathize with the stories described by the bill's supporters of the relief that smoking marijuana gives those with debilitating diseases, but I fear that New Jersey would be making a mistake with unforeseen and unintended consequences if we think we can systematically control who will have lawful access to a controlled and dangerous subject. The pitfalls are huge and the opportunity for misuse and abuse are plentiful.

The Evidence of Marijuana's Efficacy Is Lacking

The Senate committee stated that medical research suggested that smoking marijuana may alleviate pain or other symptoms associated with certain medical conditions. Yet, there have been no studies conducted by the FDA to substantiate this claim.

Further, the Multiple Sclerosis Society's Information Sourcebook—last updated in 2005—advised that "based on studies to date, it is the opinion of the National Multiple Sclerosis Society's Medical Advisory Board that there are currently insufficient data to recommend marijuana or its derivatives as a treatment for MS. Long-term use of marijuana may be associated with significant serious side effects."

New Jersey—like the other 13 states—is in the process of sidestepping the protocol for approving medications. Questions regarding the use and effectiveness of medicine are for the FDA

The US Food and Drug Administration's Position on Medical Marijuana

Claims have been advanced asserting smoked marijuana has a value in treating various medical conditions. Some have argued that herbal marijuana is a safe and effective medication and that it should be made available to people who suffer from a number of ailments upon a doctor's recommendation, even though it is not an approved drug.

Marijuana is listed in schedule I of the Controlled Substances Act (CSA), the most restrictive schedule. The Drug Enforcement Administration (DEA), which administers the CSA, continues to support that placement and FDA concurred because marijuana met the three criteria for placement in Schedule I under 21 USC. 812(b)(1) (e.g., marijuana has a high potential for abuse, has no currently accepted medical use in treatment in the United States, and has a lack of accepted safety for use under medical supervision). Furthermore, there is currently sound evidence that smoked marijuana is harmful. A past evaluation by several Department of Health and Human Services (HHS) agencies, including the Food and Drug Administration (FDA), Substance Abuse and Mental Health Services Administration (SAMHSA) and National Institute for Drug Abuse (NIDA), concluded that no sound scientific studies supported medical use of marijuana for treatment in the United States, and no animal or human data supported the safety or efficacy of marijuana for general medical use. There are alternative FDA-approved medications in existence for treatment of many of the proposed uses of smoked marijuana.

Source: "FDA Statement on Smoked Medical Marijuana," US Food and Drug Administration, April 20, 2006.

to answer, not special interest groups, not individuals, and not the state Legislature.

Legalization Is Not the Right Policy for New Jersey

I am sensitive to the pain that individuals endure from disease, but that does not make it appropriate to sanction the medical use of marijuana. The ends do not justify the means. The implications of this legislation are far-reaching, with an increased opportunity for abuse. I am not convinced that a secure system can be put into place that ensures the responsible production, delivery, and monitoring of medical marijuana.

Allowing either the patient or their caregiver to possess six marijuana plants for harvesting, or creating alternative treatment centers to dispense this product should raise a red flag to those concerned with making or executing sound public policy. The average marijuana plant can produce anywhere from 1 to 5 pounds of smokeable materials per year, resulting in a total harvest of anywhere between 6 to 30 pounds of marijuana. Who will oversee its output and ensure that patients do not overmedicate, or that the excess production is not diverted to those who use marijuana for recreational purposes? I would argue that New Jersey is opening Pandora's box by traveling down this road.

What is troubling about this legislation is the message that it sends to our youth. I have seen firsthand the devastation that drugs and alcohol bring not only to the individual who uses these products, but upon their families and friends as well. We should not be in the position of trying to justify to young people that smoking marijuana under certain circumstances is permissible, but unlawful and harmful under others.

While we are a compassionate society, there must be a balance between alleviating or managing pain, and creating a system that potentially does more harm than good. The road that medical marijuana legislation is traveling is laden with many potholes. There are too many unanswered questions regarding this serious public policy issue to justify it becoming law. And once the box is opened it will be difficult to return its contents if things do not work out.

Periodical and Internet Sources Bibliography

The following articles have been selected to supplement the diverse views presented in this chapter.

Daily News	"Federal Reclassification of Marijuana a Smart Move," December 11, 2011. www.daily newsonline.com
Patri Friedman	"Federalism and Medical Marijuana," *Reason*, September 24, 2010.
Lucia Graves	"Feds Should Reclassify Marijuana to Allow Medical Use, Governors Say," *Huffington Post*, December 1, 2011. www.huffingtonpost.com.
Thadeus Greenson	"'So Many Dimensions' to Pot Questions: Marijuana Legalization Has the Power to Rock Humboldt County, but How Is Anyone's Guess," *Times-Standard*, December 11, 2011.
Andrew Harris	"Medical Marijuana Should Be Legal in New York," *Wellsville Daily*, April 22, 2010.
Roger Parloff	"How Marijuana Became Legal," *Fortune*, September 18, 2009.
Alex Romero	"Who Says Marijuana Is Good Medicine?," *East Valley Tribune*, August 17, 2010.
Robert Sloan	"Medical Marijuana Should Be Legal," *Qondio*, March 31, 2009.
Nancy J. Thorner	"Don't Legalize Medical Marijuana," *Chicago Tribune*, February 15, 2011.
Times-News (Twin Falls, ID)	"Legalizing Medical Marijuana Means Legalizing All Marijuana," April 18, 2010. www.magicvalley .com
Gerald Turetsky	"Medical Marijuana Too Dangerous, Costly," *Times Union* (Albany, NY), June 30, 2010.

Is Medical Marijuana Good for Society?

Chapter Preface

Although a number of societies throughout history have used marijuana for medicinal purposes, it wasn't until recently that science began to investigate the drug's effectiveness in earnest. Through extensive testing and research, scientists are probing the drug's psychiatric, therapeutic, and medicinal benefits and risks. Supporters of medical marijuana view positive research studies as ammunition in the fight to legalize medical marijuana in the United States. However, many supporters of medical marijuana worry that no matter the amount of scientific evidence compiled by reputable researchers, politics will interfere in US government policy on medical marijuana.

The US government strictly controls the legal production of marijuana for medical research. As many pro-marijuana groups note, the US government does not treat other Schedule I drugs in the same manner. According to the Drug Policy Alliance, "The federal government does not retain a monopoly on the production of any other Schedule I drug, with multiple private producers having DEA [Drug Enforcement Administration] licenses to manufacture MDMA, psilocybin, etc., for sale for use in federally-approved research. In fact, the laws regulating the licensing of producers of Schedule I drugs specifically require adequate competition, the opposite of a monopoly."

This monopoly on the government's supply of legal marijuana has generated much controversy in the scientific community. Some researchers maintain that the marijuana supplied to them for testing has a low potency and is inadequate for testing; this weaker marijuana hinders the work of researchers who require a certain potency to test a certain drug or safely and effectively treat a medical condition.

Another criticism is that the National Institute on Drug Abuse (NIDA), which manages the US legal marijuana supply for testing, has turned down a number of approved studies for controversial reasons, leading some to believe that politics plays a role in deciding who can have access to medical marijuana.

In recent years, researchers and medical marijuana supporters have pressured the DEA to reclassify marijuana from a Schedule I drug to a less restricted classification. This would loosen the government's control over medical research and allow studies to utilize a stronger, more potent strain of the drug in their testing. On June 21, 2011, DEA Administrator Michele Leonhart announced the government's rejection of those calls for reclassification. The Department of Health and Human Services (DHHS), she states, "concluded that marijuana has a high potential for abuse, has no accepted medical use in the United States, and lacks an acceptable level of safety for use even under medical supervision. Therefore, DHHS recommended that marijuana remain in Schedule I."

The debate over medical marijuana's medicinal value is explored in the following chapter, which examines whether it is good for society. Other subjects discussed in the chapter include medical marijuana's societal value, its acceptance in US culture, and its connection to teen drug use.

> *"Cannabinoids have a remarkable safety record, particularly when compared to other therapeutically active substances."*

Medical Marijuana Is Safe and Has Societal Value

Paul Armentano

Paul Armentano is the deputy director of NORML (National Organization for the Reform of Marijuana Laws). In the following viewpoint, he underscores the impressive safety record of medical marijuana to treat a number of debilitating and chronic medical conditions. Armentano surveys the unprecedented scope of global research on the uses, efficacy, and safety of medical marijuana, pointing out that researchers believe the drug not only treats disease, but can also modify it. Armentano expresses hope that medical marijuana has broader applications than researchers could imagine years ago.

As you read, consider the following questions:

1. According to a 2010 German report, how many controlled studies assessing the safety and efficacy of marijuana have there been since 2005?

2. How many published papers does the author say there are on the therapeutic value of cannabinoids?

3. According to a 2005 World Health Organization review, how many recorded cases of cannabis overdose have there been?

Despite the ongoing political debate regarding the legality of medical marijuana, clinical investigations of the therapeutic use of cannabinoids are now more prevalent than at any time in history.

For example, in February 2010 investigators at the University of California Center for Medicinal Cannabis Research publicly announced the findings of a series of randomized, placebo-controlled clinical trials on the medical utility of inhaled cannabis. The studies, which utilized the so-called 'gold standard' FDA clinical trial design, concluded that marijuana ought to be a "first line treatment" for patients with neuropathy and other serious illnesses.

Among the studies conducted by the Center, four assessed smoked marijuana's ability to alleviate neuropathic pain, a notoriously difficult to treat type of nerve pain associated with cancer, diabetes, HIV/AIDS, spinal cord injury and many other debilitating conditions. Each of the trials found that cannabis consistently reduced patients' pain levels to a degree that was as good or better than currently available medications.

Another study conducted by the Center's investigators assessed the use of marijuana as a treatment for patients suffering from multiple sclerosis. That study determined that "smoked cannabis was superior to placebo in reducing spasticity and pain in patients with MS, and provided some benefit beyond currently prescribed treatments."

Global Research into Medical Marijuana

Around the globe, similarly controlled trials are also taking place. A 2010 review by researchers in Germany reports that since 2005 there have been 37 controlled studies assessing the safety and efficacy of marijuana and its naturally occurring compounds in a total of 2,563 subjects. By contrast, most FDA-approved drugs go through far fewer trials involving far fewer subjects.

While much of the renewed interest in cannabinoid therapeutics is a result of the discovery of the endocannabinoid regulatory system, some of this increased attention is also due to the growing body of testimonials from medical cannabis patients and their physicians. Nevertheless, despite this influx of anecdotal reports, much of the modern investigation of medical cannabis remains limited to preclinical (animal) studies of individual cannabinoids (e.g. THC or cannabidiol) and/or synthetic cannabinoid agonists (e.g., dronabinol or WIN 55,212-2) rather than clinical trial investigations involving whole plant material. Because of the US government's strong public policy stance against any use of cannabis, the bulk of this modern cannabinoid research is predictably taking place outside the United States.

Combating Disease

As clinical research into the therapeutic value of cannabinoids has proliferated—there are now an estimated 20,000 published papers in the scientific literature analyzing marijuana and its constituents—so too has investigators' understanding of cannabis' remarkable capability to combat disease. Whereas researchers in the 1970s, 80s, and 90s primarily assessed cannabis' ability to temporarily alleviate various disease symptoms—such as the nausea associated with cancer chemotherapy—scientists today are exploring the potential role of cannabinoids to modify disease.

Of particular interest, scientists are investigating cannabinoids' capacity to moderate autoimmune disorders such as multiple sclerosis, rheumatoid arthritis, and inflammatory bowel disease, as well as their role in the treatment of neurological disorders such as Alzheimer's disease and amyotrophic lateral sclerosis (a.k.a. Lou Gehrig's disease). In fact, in 2009, the American

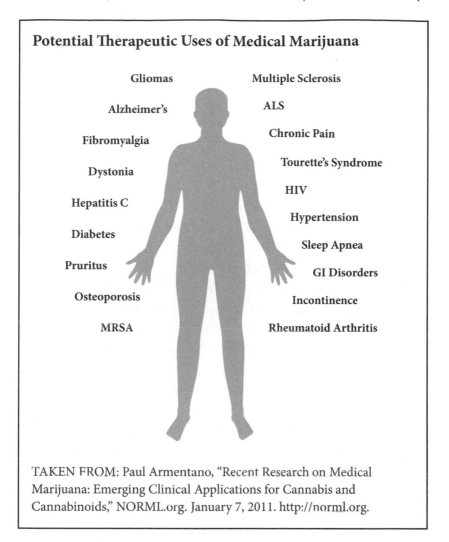

Potential Therapeutic Uses of Medical Marijuana

Gliomas	Multiple Sclerosis
Alzheimer's	ALS
Fibromyalgia	Chronic Pain
Dystonia	Tourette's Syndrome
Hepatitis C	HIV
Diabetes	Hypertension
Pruritus	Sleep Apnea
Osteoporosis	GI Disorders
MRSA	Incontinence
	Rheumatoid Arthritis

TAKEN FROM: Paul Armentano, "Recent Research on Medical Marijuana: Emerging Clinical Applications for Cannabis and Cannabinoids," NORML.org. January 7, 2011. http://norml.org.

Medical Association (AMA) resolved for the first time in the organization's history "that marijuana's status as a federal Schedule I controlled substance be reviewed with the goal of facilitating the conduct of clinical research and development of cannabinoid-based medicines."

Investigators are also studying the anti-cancer activities of cannabis, as a growing body of preclinical and clinical data concludes that cannabinoids can reduce the spread of specific cancer cells via apoptosis (programmed cell death) and by the inhibition of angiogenesis (the formation of new blood vessels). Arguably, these latter findings represent far broader and more significant applications for cannabinoid therapeutics than researchers could have imagined some thirty or even twenty years ago.

The Safety Profile of Medical Cannabis

Cannabinoids have a remarkable safety record, particularly when compared to other therapeutically active substances. Most significantly, the consumption of marijuana—regardless of quantity or potency—cannot induce a fatal overdose. According to a 1995 review prepared for the World Health Organization, "There are no recorded cases of overdose fatalities attributed to cannabis, and the estimated lethal dose for humans extrapolated from animal studies is so high that it cannot be achieved by . . . users."

In 2008, investigators at McGill University Health Centre and McGill University in Montreal and the University of British Columbia in Vancouver reviewed 23 clinical investigations of medical cannabinoid drugs (typically oral THC or liquid cannabis extracts) and eight observational studies conducted between 1966 and 2007. Investigators "did not find a higher incidence rate of serious adverse events associated with medical cannabinoid use" compared to non-using controls over these four decades.

That said, cannabis should not necessarily be viewed as a 'harmless' substance. Its active constituents may produce a variety of physiological and euphoric effects. As a result, there may be some populations that are susceptible to increased risks from the use of cannabis, such as adolescents, pregnant or nursing mothers, and patients who have a family history of mental illness. Patients with hepatitis C, decreased lung function (such as chronic obstructive pulmonary disease), or who have a history of heart disease or stroke may also be at a greater risk of experiencing adverse side effects from marijuana. As with any medication, patients should consult thoroughly with their physician before deciding whether the medical use of cannabis is safe and appropriate.

> *"Perhaps the greatest misconception from the drug legalization community is that marijuana can treat symptoms or illnesses which themselves can be the result of marijuana use."*

Medical Marijuana Is Addictive and Destructive

Brittany Farrell

Brittany Farrell is a research associate with the North Carolina Family Policy Council. In the following viewpoint, she asserts that the use of medical marijuana has medicinal risks, including respiratory illnesses, immune system complications, and mental health problems. The effects are particularly acute for young people, the author declares. Farrell also points out that the legalization of medical marijuana has complicated the issue of law enforcement and will lead to the full legalization of marijuana. For those reasons, she recommends that North Carolina legislators reject any attempt to legalize medical marijuana in the state.

As you read, consider the following questions:

1. According to the Department of Health and Human Services, how many Americans over the age of twelve have tried marijuana at least once?
2. How did smoking one marijuana cigarette every other day for a year impact an individual's white-blood-cell count, according to a Columbia University study?
3. How high does the author say that THC levels have been in some marijuana samples?

Approximately 95 million Americans over the age of 12 have tried marijuana at least once, making it the most widely used illicit drug in the United States, according to the Department of Health and Human Services. Despite the federal government's classification of marijuana as a Schedule I controlled substance, the last decade has brought increased debate regarding the possibility of legalizing the drug for medicinal purposes. While 13 American states have legalized "medical marijuana," the medical community and government are much more hesitant to jump on the bandwagon. A host of risks are associated with marijuana use from health to legal to economic. This drug is currently illegal because of the physical, social, behavioral, and academic harm it causes.

Physical Risks

Perhaps the greatest misconception from the drug legalization community is that marijuana can treat symptoms or illnesses which themselves can be the result of marijuana use. These include respiratory illnesses, immune system complications, and poor mental health. Additionally, marijuana use is known to contribute to increased violence, traffic accidents, drug abuse, as well as poor grades and risky sexual behavior in youth. The prominent chemical in marijuana, delta-9-tetrahydrocannabinol (THC), is known to obstruct the flow of chemical neurotransmitters, which are linked to both addiction and feelings of pleasure. THC affects cannabinoid receptors specifically in the parts of the brain responsible for pleasure, memory, thought, concentration, sensory time and perception, and coordinated movement.

Marijuana vs. Tobacco

A common argument in support of the legalization of marijuana for medicinal or other purposes is that it is less harmful than currently legal tobacco products, specifically cigarettes. This claim does not hold up under scrutiny, however. Almost all concerned parties are in agreement that tobacco is detrimental to both the short-term and long-term health of smokers and non-smokers who have been exposed to secondhand smoke. Unlike tobacco products, marijuana damages both the physical and mental health of users, often in much worse and more permanent ways.

Smoking three or four marijuana joints a day causes the same respiratory harm of smoking a full pack of cigarettes every day. Each joint contains between 50 and 70 percent more carcinogenic hydrocarbons than any cigarette. Marijuana also contains high levels of the enzyme known to convert hydrocarbons into malignant cells. Marijuana smokers inhale three to five times more tar and absorb three to five times more carbon monoxide than do tobacco smokers.

Marijuana is considered addictive by the American Psychiatric Association. According to its *Diagnostic and Statistical Manual of Mental Disorders*, marijuana meets criteria necessary for substance dependence including "tolerance (needing more of the substance to achieve the same effects, or diminished effect with the same amount of the substance); withdrawal symptoms; using a drug even in the presence of adverse effects; and giving up social, occupational, or recreational activities because of substance abuse." In 2002, marijuana was the substance of choice for more than 60 percent of Americans who abused or were dependent on illicit drugs.

In sum, marijuana poses significantly more risks to respiratory health than tobacco, contains much higher amounts of harmful chemicals like tar, carcinogens, and carbon monoxide found in cigarettes, and is also addictive. To date, the U.S. Food and Drug Administration (FDA) has not approved a single medication that is smoked because smoking is considered such a crude means by which to deliver medicine. Because THC may be beneficial to the treatment of some illnesses, though, researchers continue their attempts to refine the isolation of it and to develop alternative non-smoking delivery systems. Marinol is a current example of a drug successfully made from synthetic THC to treat nausea in chemotherapy patients. According to the Institute of Medicine "there is little future in smoked marijuana as a medically approved medication."

Respiratory Illnesses

Marijuana causes many of the same respiratory problems as tobacco. Coughing, wheezing, chest colds, and bronchitis are outward signs of more serious internal problems. Lung inflammation, obstructed airways, and impaired function of smaller air passages make breathing difficult. More concerning are the precancerous abnormalities and reduction in the defensive mechanisms of the lungs. According to a Harvard paper on the medical dangers of marijuana, there are an "unexpectedly large proportion of marijuana users among cases of lung cancer and cancers of the oral cavity, pharynx, and larynx." Deterioration in lung function and the lungs' abilities to defend against harmful substances or microorganisms raises the risk of lung infections.

Immunosuppressant

Advocates of "medical marijuana" see a role for marijuana in the treatment of nausea among chemotherapy patients and loss of appetite among AIDS patients. The most glaring problem with this claim is that marijuana is an immunosuppressant that weakens natural immune mechanisms, including so called "killer cells" and T-cells, which are primarily responsible for fighting infection and are already deficient in persons with either of these conditions. The same Harvard paper discussing the medical dangers of marijuana use found that marijuana may in fact "accelerate the progression of HIV to full-blown AIDS and increases the occurrence of infections," which are especially dangerous to patients with weakened immune systems as a result of AIDS or chemotherapy.

A single joint a day can so damage the cells in the bronchial passages that they are unable to protect against inhaled microorganisms making it more difficult for immune cells in the lungs to fight fungi, bacteria, and tumor cells. A Columbia University study found that smoking one marijuana cigarette every other day for a year resulted in a white-blood-cell count 39 percent lower than normal. This significant drop is likely fatal for patients with already weakened immune systems. There is no wisdom in prescribing marijuana for patients who cannot afford another attack on their immune system.

Mental Health

Despite claims that marijuana is less harmful than cocaine, heroin, and alcohol, it exhibits similar brain changes as each of these other substances. Cognitive impairment, distorted perception, memory loss, trouble with thinking and problem solving, difficulty learning, anxiety, panic attacks, depression, social withdrawal, paranoia, and hallucinations are just the beginning of the mental health complications presented by marijuana use. These symptoms can last as long as six weeks after the last use of the drug. Ironically, panic attacks are one of the conditions marijuana advocates are experimentally treating with the drug.

The American Psychiatric Association is so concerned about this aspect of mental health that the *Diagnostic and Statistical Manual of Mental Disorders (DSM) IV* contains a complete section for mental disorders connected to marijuana use. These categories include "Cannabis Intoxication (consisting of impaired motor coordination, anxiety, impaired judgment, sensation of slowed time, social withdrawal . . .); Cannabis Intoxication Delirium (memory deficit, disorientation); Cannabis Induced Psychotic Disorder, Delusions; Cannabis Induced Psychotic Disorder, Hallucinations; and Cannabis Induced Anxiety Disorder." Addiction and psychiatric disorders often occur together, according to the American Society of Addiction Medicine. Research on the effect of marijuana on mental health points to the same conclusion.

Youth

Due to the overwhelming data on the especially adverse impact of marijuana use on youth, even supporters of the drug do not want kids using it. Still, 42 percent of American high school students had used marijuana at least once, according to the 2001 Youth Risk Behavior Surveillance System. Smoking marijuana is one of the worst things youth can do. There is a clear relationship between academic performance and drug use. Students with a D average are four times as likely to have recently used marijuana as students with an A average. Poor performance in school takes the form of "deficits in mathematical skills and verbal expression," as well as memory-retrieval processes.

By lowering inhibitions about drug use and exposing youth to the drug culture which encourage use of other drugs, marijuana truly does act as a "gateway drug" for adolescents. The *Journal of the American Medical Association* reported a study of 300 sets of twins that showed that the twins who used marijuana were four times more likely to go on to use cocaine or crack cocaine and were five times more likely to use such hallucinogens as LSD. Drug use among adolescents also leads to dependence triple the incidence of dependence among adults.

Marijuana use leads to more reckless lifestyles for adolescents. Smokers of the drug are three times as likely to consider committing suicide. A 2003 Canadian study reported approximately 20 percent of students drive within an hour of using mar-

"Wish I could!"

ijuana. Even moderate doses of marijuana slow reaction time, distort perception, and impair motor skills. Finally, youths who use marijuana tend to have more unprotected sex with more partners beginning at a younger age.

Legal Implications

The legal obstacles posed by the legalization of marijuana for medical purposes arise primarily as a result of a discrepancy between federal and state law and logistical difficulties in enforcing and regulating standards. The Comprehensive Drug Abuse Prevention and Control Act of 1970 established marijuana as a Schedule I controlled substance. Substances under this category are illegal to possess, distribute, or use and "are categorized as such because of their high potential for abuse, lack of any accepted medical use, and absence of any accepted safety for use in medically supervised treatment." The 13 states that have "legalized" marijuana for medical or other purposes have done nothing more than attempt to provide a small defense for anyone caught with marijuana in those states. Federal law still considers marijuana an illegal substance and law enforcement officials can and will charge citizens accordingly, regardless of state law. The British Medical Association in 2004 voiced "extreme concern" that efforts to downgrade the criminal status of marijuana would give the public a false sense of security about the safety of the drug when, "in fact, it has been linked to greater risk of heart disease, lung cancer, bronchitis, and emphysema" among other conditions.

Despite proponents' arguments that the legalization of marijuana would allow for better government regulation and increased revenue through taxation, legalization has done little more than add to the problems of law enforcement in states like California. Marijuana has to be grown somewhere. Public lands like national forests and parks have become breeding grounds for massive crop growth and organized crime. This poses a serious threat to the security of citizens and tourists in these areas. It is common for illegal Asian and South American nationals to be hired by drug cartels as armed guards with orders to shoot anyone threatening this major cash crop, especially rival cartels and including law enforcement officers. These lands are enticing because they are "free and accessible, crop ownership is hard to document, and because growers are immune to asset forfeiture laws." However, there is a substantial threat to public safety, when playgrounds and natural recreation areas for families and children are caught in the midst of a gang fight over territory for growing this unhealthy and illegal drug.

Quality control is a serious concern when considering any medication, but is even more of a concern for a substance with the number and diversity of health risks associated with marijuana. So far, no state has been able to fashion a law that sufficiently allows for regulation of the quality of the drug before being given to patients because it is so easy for individuals to grow and exchange small or large quantities of marijuana undetected. Because marijuana is illegal in the United States, even in states that wish to treat it as legal, doctors are not able to prescribe it like a typical drug with dosage instructions. This means that there is no control over the consumption of the drug by anyone from legitimate patients to addicted users. As the Office of National Drug Control Policy points out, "medicines are not approved in this country by popular vote," but that is exactly how marijuana has come to be not only debated but used as a legitimate medicine.

Economic Drain

The impacts on the physical and mental health of users of marijuana lead to lower school and job performance, thereby robbing both the individual and society of the fruits of their labor. Additionally, the negative health impacts result in additional strain on an already stretched and expensive health care system.

However, the production and distribution of marijuana itself requires high opportunity costs. In California, individual growers or drug cartels buy or rent houses for the expressed purpose of using them to grow large quantities of marijuana, thereby making the homes unlivable and virtually worthless after the crop is harvested. In addition, these cartels already "smuggle hundreds of undocumented Mexican nationals" to help grow, guard, harvest, and distribute the drug. This practice directly contributes to the hotly debated issue of illegal immigration and its costs to the American public.

Faulty Advertising

Proponents of legalizing marijuana have a dirty little secret about their motives. The movement is not merely an effort to legalize marijuana for legitimate medical use. Many organizations like the Drug Policy Alliance, the National Organization for the Reform of Marijuana Laws, and the Lindesmith Center do not deny using "medical marijuana" as "a stalking horse for drug legalization" more generally and beginning with marijuana.

The "medical marijuana" movement targets youth through pro-drug messages on television, in movies, in books and magazines, and in music. The White House Office of National Drug Control Policy asserts that "More often than not, the culture glamorizes or trivializes marijuana use and fails to portray the harm it can cause." The internet, where young people disproportionately spend their time, is especially rife with websites touting the wonders of marijuana, selling kits to beat drug tests, and advertising marijuana for sale.

What is so dangerous is that the pot of today is not the pot of the 1960s or 1970s. The average amount of THC has jumped from less than one percent to over six percent in the last 30 years. Some samples have been found to contain THC levels reaching 33 percent. Because of this increased potency, users today face more damage that is done faster and with significantly less exposure to marijuana.

North Carolina's Stance on Medical Marijuana

Thus far, the state of North Carolina has avoided much consideration or debate on the subject of "medical marijuana." However, during the 2008 short session of the NC General Assembly, House Bill 2405—LRC Study/Alternative Medicines was introduced by Representative Earl Jones (D-Guilford). Introduced a mere 12 days after the Office of National Drug Control Policy (ONDCP) issued its report, "Teen Marijuana Use Worsens Depression: An Analysis of Recent Data Shows 'Self-Medicating' Could Actually Make Things Worse," the bill asked the Legislative Research Commission to study the "possible public benefits of allowing marijuana or its chemical equivalent to be used for medicinal purposes." This despite the fact that the ONDCP report found that "using marijuana can worsen depression and lead to serious mental health disorders, such as schizophrenia, anxiety, and even suicide." The bill never made it out of committee and therefore died. Similar bills have been filed in previous sessions but were not considered.

North Carolina should continue to heed the warnings regarding the physical, social, behavioral, and academic harm caused by marijuana and refuse to give credence to opportunistic individuals. There is no such thing as "medical marijuana" and North Carolina should refuse to jeopardize the health and safety of all her citizens by abiding by federal law which has classified marijuana as a dangerous Schedule I substance for good reasons.

[For a footnoted version of this article, please visit ncfamily.org.]

"Smoked marijuana has the potential to help those individuals who do not benefit from, or can not tolerate, currently available therapies."

Marijuana Effectively Treats a Number of Health Conditions

Center for Health and Pharmaceutical Law and Policy, Seton Hall University School of Law

The Center for Health and Pharmaceutical Law and Policy researches health and legal issues at the Seton Hall University School of Law. In the following viewpoint, the center outlines the medicinal value of marijuana, finding it to be a widely accepted option for treating a number of debilitating medical conditions. It also praises New Jersey's proposed law to legalize medical marijuana, the New Jersey Compassionate Use Medical Marijuana Act, for including a number of safeguards to prevent abuse and diversion of medical marijuana. Further research is needed to fully explore the drug's medicinal potential, the center concludes.

As you read, consider the following questions:

1. According to the American College of Physicians, what primary active ingredient in marijuana is particularly effective as an appetite stimulant?
2. According to a 2008 *European Journal of Cancer Care* survey, cannabinoid drugs were more effective than standard anti-nausea drugs in alleviating what symptoms that accompany chemotherapy?
3. How long does smoked marijuana take to reach its peak level in a patient's blood, according to studies cited in the viewpoint?

Medical evidence supports the use of marijuana to relieve symptoms or ameliorate the side effects of primary treatments of each of the debilitating medical conditions set forth in the [New Jersey Compassionate Use Medical Marijuana] Act: AIDS/HIV; cachexia (wasting syndrome); cancer; glaucoma; severe and persistent muscle spasms; severe nausea; severe or chronic pain; and seizures. While conventional treatments are available for some of these conditions for some patients, smoked marijuana has the potential to help those individuals who do not benefit from, or can not tolerate, currently available therapies.

AIDS/HIV and Wasting Syndrome

Marijuana is an effective treatment for cachexia, also known as wasting syndrome, an involuntary loss of appetite and weight linked to disease progression and death in patients with AIDS/ HIV. The American College of Physicians has concluded that abundant support exists for the use of the cannabinoid delta-9-tetrahydrocannabinol ("THC"), one of the primary active ingredients in marijuana, as an appetite stimulant. The FDA concurs, as evidenced by its approval of Marinol, a pill containing a synthetic version of THC, to treat "anorexia associated with weight loss in patients with AIDS."

Marijuana is also an effective treatment for AIDS/HIV-associated sensory neuropathy, a condition characterized by excruciating pain in the nerve endings that afflicts over a third of patients with AIDS/HIV. In the past two years, three placebo-controlled, randomized, double-blind clinical trials published in the medical literature have demonstrated that smoked marijuana is effective against neuropathic pain, including for patients who have tried the available conventional treatments and are still in pain. The available treatments for AIDS/HIV-associated neuropathic pain fail to help large numbers of those who suffer from it. Neither aspirin-like drugs nor anti-depressants help, and even opioids are of limited efficacy. Anti-convulsant drugs have been found effective in treating the condition, but some patients do not respond to them and others can not tolerate them. For these reasons, marijuana, which does not increase HIV viral load or decrease CD4 cell counts, could be an important addition to the pharmaceutical armamentarium for treating the chronic neuropathic pain of patients with AIDS/HIV.

Cancer and Severe Nausea

Marijuana is also an effective treatment for the severe nausea and vomiting that can accompany cancer treatment. A 2008 review published in the *European Journal of Cancer Care* analyzed 30 clinical studies and concluded that cannabinoid drugs were more effective than standard antinausea drugs in alleviating the nausea and vomiting that accompanies chemotherapy. In addition, the FDA has approved both the Marinol and Cesamet pills, which contain synthetic chemical compounds equivalent or similar to THC, to treat nausea and vomiting associated with cancer chemotherapy for patients who have not responded adequately to conventional antiemetic treatments.

Glaucoma

Intraocular pressure (fluid pressure in the eyes) is the most important risk factor for glaucoma, a leading cause of blindness.

Scientists have long known that smoking marijuana lowers intraocular pressure in glaucoma patients. Marijuana is not generally recommended as a treatment for glaucoma, because the available conventional treatments are both longer-acting and have fewer side effects. Marijuana may provide relief to some glaucoma patients for whom conventional treatments are ineffective or intolerable, however.

Severe and Persistent Muscle Spasms

Many multiple sclerosis ("MS") patients suffer from painful muscle spasms which have a major negative influence on their quality of life. A prospective, randomized, placebo-controlled crossover trial in adults with MS established smoked marijuana's superiority to placebo in reducing spasticity and pain. In March 2009, the manufacturer of Sativex, an oral spray containing THC and cannabidiol, another cannabinoid extracted from marijuana, announced highly statistically-significant preliminary positive results from a placebo-controlled, randomized, double-blind trial of Sativex for the treatment of spasticity in MS patients for whom existing therapies have not produced relief. Previous studies of Sativex provide additional support for its effectiveness as a treatment for spasticity and other symptoms of MS.

A large, randomized, placebo-controlled clinical trial showed a small, non-statistically-significant improvement in spasticity, as measured by the Ashworth Spasticity Scale, in MS patients who took pills containing either cannabis extract or THC. Study participants who took cannabis extract or THC pills also experienced objective improvement in mobility and reported subjective improvement in pain, sleep quality, and spasms and spasticity. A year-long follow-up clinical trial of patients who chose to recommence taking their study medication showed a small, statistically-significant improvement in spasticity as measured by the Ashworth Scale in those who took pills containing THC.

Severe or Chronic Pain

In addition to the evidence discussed above supporting the use of marijuana as a treatment for neuropathic pain, recent studies show that cannabinoids are an effective treatment for other forms of severe or chronic pain including cancer pain, multiple sclerosis pain, and rheumatoid arthritis pain. In 2003, the authors of an article in *The Lancet* concluded that cannabinoids "inhibit pain in virtually every experimental pain paradigm . . . in supra-spinal, spinal, or peripheral regions depending on the type of nociceptive pathway being studied." The Mayo Clinic concludes that THC may work as well as the opiate drug codeine in treating cancer pain. Opiates, such as codeine and morphine, are not consistently effective against chronic pain, in part because tolerance occurs in some patients (meaning that they need an ever-increasing dose to get the same therapeutic effect). Opiates can also have undesirable side effects including nausea and sedation. Notably, cannabinoids appear to enhance the effects of opiate pain medications, enabling patients to obtain relief at lower dosages and thereby minimize side effects.

Seizures

The results of the only controlled clinical trial of a cannabinoid for the treatment of epilepsy to be published in the medical literature suggest that oral cannabidiol has promise as a treatment for the 20–30% of epileptics whose symptoms are inadequately controlled by conventional medication. Of the eight patients in the study who received oral cannabidiol, four were virtually seizure free and three others exhibited improvement. By comparison, six out of the seven patients who received the placebo treatment failed to improve. In addition, multiple anecdotal reports support the efficacy of smoked marijuana as a treatment for epilepsy. These reports reveal that in individuals who smoke marijuana to control their epilepsy, stopping smoking leads to the reemergence of seizures.

Smoked Marijuana Has Advantages over Cesamet and Marinol Pills

Although smoking carries with it certain health risks, smoked marijuana has meaningful advantages over Cesamet and Marinol, the pills containing synthetic cannabinoids currently available in the United States, and over Sativex, the oral spray containing marijuana extracts which is not available in this country.

First, smoked marijuana is faster acting than either the pills or the spray. Smoked cannabis reaches its peak level in a patient's blood within minutes; the pills can take from one to six hours to reach the same level. Sativex spray has better pharmokinetics than the Cesamet and Marinol pills, but still does not compare favorably to smoked marijuana.

Second, smoked marijuana allows for more reliable dosing than the pills. With smoked marijuana, patients can take in as much as they need to achieve relief and no more; this is impossible with the pills. In addition, the pills' effectiveness varies, leaving patients without predictable relief from their symptoms.

Third, the pills have more pronounced, much longer-lasting psychoactive side effects, including dysphoria, intoxication, and sedation, than smoked marijuana. This is in part because patients who smoke marijuana are better able to adjust their dose to avoid side effects, but also because of the way that the orally-ingested pills are metabolized in the gastrointestinal tract.

Finally, smoked marijuana may be the only viable option for patients who can not swallow pills due to severe nausea and vomiting, for example as a result of treatment for cancer.

An Endorsement of Smoked Marijuana

The Institute of Medicine (IOM), in its comprehensive 1999 report "Marijuana and Medicine: Assessing the Science Base," endorsed short-term use of smoked marijuana in cases in which all approved medications have failed and it is reasonably likely to be effective. While the IOM declined to endorse long-term medical use of smoked marijuana because of the health risks associated

Physicians and Medical Marijuana

A 1991 Harvard study found that 44 percent of oncologists had previously advised marijuana therapy to their patients. Fifty percent responded they would do so if marijuana was legal. A more recent national survey performed by researchers at Providence Rhode Island Hospital found that nearly half of physicians with opinions supported legalizing medical marijuana.

Source: "Medical Use," National Organization for the Reform of Marijuana Laws, 2011. http://norml.org.

with smoking, it conceded that for certain patients, such as the terminally ill or those with debilitating symptoms, the long-term risks are not of great concern. Whether the advantages of smoked marijuana outweigh the health risks associated with smoking is a decision best made by those suffering from debilitating medical conditions and their physicians.

Abuse and Diversion

Other states' experiences with medical marijuana laws can help quell any fear that passing the Act could lead to an increase in recreational marijuana use in New Jersey. As noted above, no state that has passed a medical marijuana law has subsequently experienced an increase in recreational marijuana use among its children and youth. In California (which has the nation's most permissive medical marijuana law), a biennial survey conducted by the California Attorney General shows that marijuana use by young people declined markedly in the decade following passage of that law. Providing further reassurance is the fact that the New Jersey Compassionate Use Medical Marijuana Act incorporates multiple safeguards to prevent abuse and diversion of medical marijuana. In fact, if passed, the Act would be among the most restrictive of all the states' medical marijuana laws.

To minimize the risk of abuse and diversion of medical marijuana, the Act requires every prospective patient to apply to the Department of Health and Senior Services ("DHSS") for a mandatory "registry identification card." The card, which would include the patient's photograph, would provide proof of DHSS approval; without it, the statute would provide no protection. Before issuing a card, DHSS would be required to verify all of the information in a prospective patient's application.

Safeguards

Patients would need to demonstrate to DHHS that they qualify for the Act's protection by producing medical records or the recommendation of a physician with whom they have a bona-fide physician-patient relationship. The physician would have to sign a statement attesting to his or her professional opinion that the patient has one of the debilitating medical conditions set forth in the Act, that recognized drugs or treatments are not or would not be effective, and that the potential benefits of marijuana use likely outweigh the risks. Notably, there is no catch all category of debilitating medical conditions, as there is, for example, in California's Proposition 215, which allows for the use of medical marijuana to treat "any other illness for which marijuana provides relief." The New Jersey Act's protections are limited to patients suffering from one of the enumerated conditions.

The Act also places limits on patients' ability to obtain assistance with their possession and use of marijuana from a caregiver. Prospective patients would be required to designate in a written document on file with DHSS a single primary caregiver to possess marijuana on their behalf. The person designated as primary caregiver must be an adult who has never been convicted of a felony drug offense and who has agreed to assist with the patient's use of marijuana. A primary caregiver can only serve one patient at a time and can not also be that patient's physician. Those under 18 can only be approved to use marijuana if their parent consents and agrees to serve as their primary caregiver and to control the patients' acquisition and use of marijuana.

In addition, the Act restricts New Jersey residents' ability to produce marijuana for medical use. The Act would establish a mechanism for "medical marijuana alternative treatment centers" to seek and obtain authorization from DHSS to produce marijuana for medical purposes. DHSS would be provided with, among other information, (i) the names of the individuals operating a prospective center, (ii) the names of its employees and volunteers, (iii) the location of the center, and (iv) the registration card number of each patient whom the center will serve. Centers would be required to report a change in any of this information to DHSS within 10 days. Individuals convicted of possession or sale of a controlled dangerous substance (other than medical marijuana) would not be eligible to establish or work at an alternative treatment center. As with prospective patients, DHSS would subject prospective centers to intensive vetting, verifying the information in every permit application prior to approval.

Finally, the Act strictly limits the amount of marijuana possessed by a patient, his or her caregiver, and his or her alternative treatment center to a small total of just six plants and one ounce of usable marijuana per patient.

Recommendations

The Seton Hall Law School Center for Health and Pharmaceutical Law and Policy recommends passage of the New Jersey Compassionate Use Medical Marijuana Act because the Act includes multiple measures designed to reduce the risk of abuse or diversion and because the medical literature supports the conclusion that smoked marijuana can provide relief to patients suffering from debilitating medical conditions for whom conventional treatments have failed. While further research is needed to fully explore marijuana's medicinal potential, New Jersey residents, in consultation with their physicians, should have access to the relief from suffering that the Act would afford now.

> *"The DEA concluded that marijuana
> has no accepted medical use . . .
> because its chemistry is not known and
> adequate studies have not been done
> on its usefulness or safety."*

Marijuana Has No Proven Medical Value

John Hoeffel

John Hoeffel is a reporter for the Los Angeles Times. *In the following viewpoint, he reports that the US Drug Enforcement Administration (DEA) recently turned down a request by medical marijuana advocates to reclassify marijuana as a less dangerous drug that has an accepted medical use. The federal government's position is that marijuana is unsafe, has a high potential for abuse, and has no proven medical value. Medical marijuana supporters dispute the government's findings, and look to appeal the decision.*

As you read, consider the following questions:
1. Why does Hoeffel state that advocates for the medical use of marijuana were elated that the Obama administration finally decided on the petition?

2. How many times have petitions to reclassify marijuana been spurned by the federal government, according to Hoeffel?
3. In what year did a commission recommend that marijuana be decriminalized in the United States, according to Hoeffel?

Marijuana has been approved by California, many other states and the nation's capital to treat a range of illnesses, but in a decision announced Friday [July 8, 2011] the federal government ruled that it has no accepted medical use and should remain classified as a highly dangerous drug like heroin.

The decision comes almost nine years after medical marijuana supporters asked the government to reclassify cannabis to take into account a growing body of worldwide research that shows its effectiveness in treating certain diseases, such as glaucoma and multiple sclerosis.

Next Steps

Advocates for the medical use of the drug criticized the ruling but were elated that the Obama administration has finally acted, which allows them to appeal to the federal courts. The decision to deny the request was made by the U.S. Drug Enforcement Administration and comes less than two months after advocates asked the U.S. Court of Appeals to force the administration to respond to their petition.

"We have foiled the government's strategy of delay, and we can now go head-to-head on the merits," said Joe Elford, the chief counsel for Americans for Safe Access and the lead attorney on the lawsuit.

Elford said he was not surprised by the decision, which comes after the Obama administration announced it would not tolerate large-scale commercial marijuana cultivation. "It is clearly motivated by a political decision that is anti-marijuana," he said. He noted that studies demonstrate pot has beneficial effects, including appetite stimulation for people undergoing chemotherapy. "One of the things people say about marijuana is that it gives you the munchies and the truth is that it does, and for some people that's a very positive thing."

The US Government's Position

In a June 21 letter to the organizations that filed the petition, DEA Administrator Michele M. Leonhart said she rejected the request because marijuana "has a high potential for abuse," "has no currently accepted medical use in treatment in the United States" and "lacks accepted safety for use under medical supervision." The letter and 37 pages of supporting documents were published Friday in the Federal Register.

This is the third time that petitions to reclassify marijuana have been spurned. The first was filed in 1972 and denied 17 years later. The second was filed in 1995 and denied six years later. Both decisions were appealed, but the courts sided with the federal government.

The Coalition for Rescheduling Cannabis filed its petition in October 2002. In 2004, the DEA asked the Department of Health and Human Services to review the science. The department recommended in 2006 that marijuana remain classified as a dangerous drug. Four and a half years then elapsed before the current administration issued a final denial.

"The regulatory process is just a time-consuming one that usually takes years to go through," said Barbara Carreno, a spokeswoman for the Drug Enforcement Administration.

Recent Marijuana Research

The DEA's decision comes as researchers continue to identify beneficial effects. Dr. Igor Grant, a neuropsychiatrist who is the director of the Center for Medicinal Cannabis Research at UC San Diego, said state-supported clinical trials show that marijuana helps with neuropathic pain and muscle spasticity. He said the federal government's position discourages scientists from

US Government's Position on Reclassifying Marijuana

Based on the DHHS [Department of Health and Human Services] evaluation and all other relevant data, DEA [Drug Enforcement Administration] has concluded that . . . marijuana continues to meet the criteria for schedule I control under the CSA [Controlled Substances Act] because:

- *Marijuana has a high potential for abuse.* The DHHS evaluation and the additional data gathered by DEA show that marijuana has a high potential for abuse.

- *Marijuana has no currently accepted medical use in treatment in the United States.* . . . The drug's chemistry is not known and reproducible; there are no adequate safety studies; there are no adequate and well-controlled studies proving efficacy; the drug is not accepted by qualified experts; and the scientific evidence is not widely available.

- *Marijuana lacks accepted safety for use under medical supervision.* At present, there are no U.S. Food and Drug Administration (FDA)–approved marijuana products, nor is marijuana under a New Drug Application (NDA) evaluation at the FDA for any indication. Marijuana does not have a currently accepted medical use in treatment in the United States or a currently accepted medical use with severe restrictions. At this time, the known risks of marijuana use have not been shown to be outweighed by specific benefits in well-controlled clinical trials that scientifically evaluate safety and efficacy.

Source: Michele M. Leonhart, Denial of Petition to Initiate Proceedings to Reschedule Marijuana, Department of Justice, June 21, 2011.

pursuing research needed to test the drug's medical effectiveness. "We're trapped in kind of a vicious cycle here," he said. "It's always a danger if the government acts on certain kinds of persuasions or beliefs rather than evidence."

Popular Opinion

Popular opinion has also swung behind medical marijuana. Americans overwhelmingly support it in national polls. When the petition was filed, eight states had approved medical marijuana. Now 16 states and the District of Columbia have done so. In 2009, the American Medical Assn. urged the government to review its classification of marijuana "with the goal of facilitating the conduct of clinical research and development of cannabinoid-based medicines, and alternate delivery methods."

When Congress passed the Controlled Substances Act in 1970, it listed marijuana as a Schedule I drug, the most restrictive of five categories. But some federal officials have questioned that decision. In 1972, a commission recommended that marijuana be decriminalized. And in 1988, a DEA administrative law judge concluded that "marijuana has been accepted as capable of relieving the distress of great numbers of very ill people." The National Cancer Institute, which is part of the Department of Health and Human Services, notes that marijuana may help with nausea, loss of appetite, pain and insomnia.

Nonetheless, the DEA concluded that marijuana has no accepted medical use, Leonhart wrote in her letter, because its chemistry is not known and adequate studies have not been done on its usefulness or safety. "At this time," she said, "the known risks of marijuana use have not been shown to be outweighed by specific benefits in well-controlled clinical trials that scientifically evaluate safety and efficacy."

> *"Google medical marijuana and you will find a cross section of articles in every mainstream newspaper and magazine."*

Medical Marijuana Is Widely Accepted and Used in US Society

Norm Kent

Norm Kent is an attorney and blogger. In the following viewpoint, he observes that medical marijuana has gone mainstream in US popular culture and is widely accepted for its medicinal value by the American people. Kent says polls show that increasing numbers of Americans do not believe that people suffering from debilitating and chronic conditions should be persecuted for or prohibited from using marijuana to treat their symptoms. Kent views the recent trend for legalizing medical marijuana as a wave sweeping the country—one that will likely lead to the full legalization of marijuana.

As you read, consider the following questions:
1. What percentage of Fox News viewers endorses the Obama administration's decision to stop targeting

medical dispensaries in California, according to the viewpoint?
2. How does the author describe the government plan known as Compassionate Use Protocol?
3. According to the author, what job was the *Denver Westword* advertising for recently?

A whopping 63% of Fox News viewers have endorsed the Obama Administration's decision to stop targeting medical dispensaries in California. The disclosure was made by Geraldo Rivera last week on his popular show, 'Geraldo at Large.' For once, Fox is catching up with the rest of the nation.

Geraldo presented more than just a fair and balanced report. The news item clearly distinguished the marked differences between the casual user of marijuana for recreational or personal medical use and traffickers operating illegal Mexican drug cartels, which everyone acknowledged should be targeted for enhanced enforcement. Rivera even applauded Attorney General Eric Holder for his new and rededicated efforts to stop that illegality, inserting into his news report the AG's announcement of a raid last week, which netted 300 suspects nationwide.

Ann Coulter, of course, came on to criticize Obama, but she is a howler monkey who stands on the end of the branch and shrieks at anything Barack and Friends do or do not do. Even she had a hard time coming down too hard on smokers, preferring to just attack President Obama. Surprise. When Geraldo then turned to conservative Mike Huckabee for a countervailing viewpoint, he tempered his criticism of the new policy by recognizing that every governor has to set its priorities. The best objection he came up with was that if the Obama administration wanted to "change the law, go ahead and change it, but don't keep a law you are not going to enforce." That is a far cry from stating this was bad policy, a poor change, and counter-productive to our nation.

The Tide Is Turning for Medical Marijuana

What viewers eventually saw on the piece Geraldo did was a presentation that medical marijuana is a wave sweeping over our land, and the 15 states which already provide for it are a precursor to a national future. You could almost sense that was the direction Geraldo was headed when he opened with a segue featuring Tommy Chong and Cheech Marin at a recent 'Smoke Out' rally in LA.

Afterwards, Rivera followed with a short piece about a white-collared businessman, explaining to the audience that he ran a lawful, state-compliant dispensary which was busted by the feds. That gentleman, Phil Smith, then explained how he had just spent ten months in jail with hardened criminals and murderers. That too is a far cry from the day and time when marijuana growers were presented to American audiences as hardened criminals. Geraldo even scoffed at the way we once thought of marijuana, with a scene from *Reefer Madness* [a 1936 anti-marijuana propaganda film] dropped onto the set in the background.

As he waded through the piece on medical and legal pot, Geraldo even postured this was an issue that crossed ideological lines; that Americans across the board do not want pot law enforced harshly against our citizens. Coming from the barrios of New York City, having grown up in the 1960's, and spending decades with celebrities in the media, Geraldo uniquely understands how pervasive and personal marijuana is in the American psyche. In fact, as he recovers from knee replacement surgery, I would not be surprised if instead of using Percocet daily he tried out some Purple Haze. (I don't know, I'm just saying . . .)

The bottom line is Geraldo is one of America's grittiest and most seasoned journalists, who has covered stories from mistreatment in mental institutions to mass murders. He knows where 'pot' fits into the scheme of things—enough so that he could joke and poke at this story, recognizing as he does our nation has greater issues, more pressing problems.

The Growth of the Medical Marijuana Industry

- A national market for medical marijuana is worth $1.7 billion in 2011 and could reach $8.9 billion in five years.

- Two states, California and Colorado, dominate this nascent industry, combining to represent 92% of the wholesale and retail sales across the country. California enjoys the largest market size at $1.3 billion, while Colorado hosts the fastest growing and most business-friendly market.

- Nine other states and the District of Columbia with medical marijuana laws have or are forming active markets. Arizona, Michigan and Washington are particularly well-positioned as the industry matures in the next few years.

- There are 24.8 million potential patients eligible for medical marijuana under current state laws.

- Medical marijuana businesses face significant challenges including unfavorable tax status and downward pricing pressure but can expect high growth driven by rising new patient adoption.

- State regulations and federal policy uncertainty are the largest determinants of market activity and investment around the country.

Source: See Change Strategy, "The State of the Medical Marijuana Markets 2011," 2011.
www.mpp.org.

Compassionate Use Protocol

When NORML [National Organization for the Reform of Marijuana Laws] recently held its annual convention in San Francisco, former Mayor Willie Brown opined that "we should legalize pot because as many people are using it recreationally as are using it medically." Prop 215 author, activist Denis Peron, once stated: "all use is medical." Last year, NORML's founder, Keith Stroup, and Rick Cusick, the Publisher of *High Times*, along with 50 students from local colleges, were foolishly arrested for smoking joints at a 'MassCann(abis)' convention in the Boston Commons. The next thing you know Mr. Stroup was testifying before Massachusetts legislative committees to change the laws in the Bay State. Those statutes have now been amended to provide for the medicinal use of marijuana.

One of my clients, Elvy Mussika, is amongst the last of those getting marijuana from the United States government on a now abandoned program entitled the 'Compassionate Use Protocol.' Under the plan, the DEA grows experimental marijuana at the University of Mississippi and freeze-dries it for distribution in a prescription can to Ms. Mussika, a grandmother fighting the intraocular pressures associated with Glaucoma, which constantly cause pain in her eyes. 'Smoke 3x daily, or as needed for pain' the jar reads. There are thousands and thousands of other Americans similarly situated, who only want to use pot to relieve pain. For them, marijuana is medicine.

Pot Goes Mainstream

Then there are the Michael Phelps of the world, using bongs and water pipes and rolling papers to get high and give themselves a buzz, for fun's sake. They too should not be criminalized or denied scholarships to school, should they? Some may not win gold medals in swimming pools, but they should not be posting bail in county jails, either. They may not find themselves as guests of the *Jay Leno Show*, but they should not find themselves as guests of the local sheriff either, should they? It is becoming so normal to smoke, talk, and write about pot that NORML now represents the silent majority of Americans who just want to be left alone with their pot. It would seem that even Fox News agrees.

Google medical marijuana and you will find a cross section of articles in every mainstream newspaper and magazine. As a matter of fact, medical marijuana is becoming so 'ordinary' a story that it has found its way to cover stories in the past few months in magazines from *Forbes* to *Harper's Monthly*, not to mention the *New York Times*. Last month, *The Today Show*, with Matt Lauer as the interviewer, ran a positive news feature featuring 'Women and Pot in the Workplace.' Think about it, one of America's most popular shows presenting marijuana as medicine in a fair and unfrenzied light. Congressman Barney Frank has even postured that medical marijuana may soon become the law of the land.

In Colorado, a state which has opted for the opening of dispensaries, the *Denver Westword*, a popular newsweekly, has published a classified ad seeking to hire a random 'marijuana critic,' in order to 'taste-test' the product which its new dispensaries will be distributing. Lots of daily journalists are out of work. I am guessing there will be no shortage of applications for that job.

What is the outcome of all this to be?

Do not be surprised when a consumer affairs television reporter one day, in a neighborhood near you unveils a feature on the best marijuana dispensaries in your hometown. Medical marijuana is coming to Main Street. We are not just Zig-Zag [a brand of cigarette rolling papers associated with marijuana smoking] anymore.

> *"If you are simply alive, there is a good chance you have at least one symptom that warrants a medical marijuana card."*

Medical Marijuana Is Overprescribed

Emily Gibson

Emily Gibson is a physician and blogger. In the following viewpoint, she concedes that marijuana has some valid medicinal uses but that it is being prescribed too quickly in states where it is legal. Gibson worries that patients are too trusting of medical marijuana and that many exaggerate symptoms to get legal access to the drug. She also believes that the medical marijuana industry is filled with hucksters looking to make a profit. Gibson claims that she has seen marijuana ruin lives because it allows young people to disengage with the world around them and numb themselves to emotion for long periods of time.

As you read, consider the following questions:

1. What is Marinol, according to Gibson?

2. According to Gibson, how much can a physician pocket for a ten-minute assessment of symptoms in exchange for a signature on a medical marijuana card?
3. Where does Gibson rank marijuana on the list of problem recreational drugs?

It was 1978 and I was a third year medical student when my friend was slowly dying of metastatic breast cancer.

Her deteriorating cervical spine, riddled with tumor, was stabilized by a metal halo drilled into her skull and attached to a scaffolding-like contraption resting on her shoulders. Vomiting while immobilized in a halo became a form of medieval torture. During her third round of chemotherapy, her nausea was so unrelenting that none of the conventional medications available at the time would give her relief. She was in and out of the hospital multiple times for rehydration with intravenous fluids, but her desire was to be home with her husband and children for the days left to her on this earth.

Her family doctor, at his wit's end, finally recommended she try marijuana for her nausea. My friend was willing to try anything at that point, so one of her college age children located a using friend, bought some bud and brought it home.

Smoking, because of its relatively rapid effects, it didn't do much other than make her feel "out of it" so that she was less aware of her family, and she hated that the entire house reeked of weed, especially as she still had two teenage children still at home. Her nausea prevented her from eating marijuana mixed into brownies or cookies.

Taking Action

Desperate times called for desperate measures. I simmered the marijuana in a small amount of water to soften it, then combined it with melted butter. That mixture was chilled until it was solid and I molded multiple bullet size suppositories, which were kept in the freezer until needed for rectal administration. Although we never could warm up the suppositories to a temperature that was comfortable for her without them melting into unusable marijuana mush, she found that she could get relief from the nausea within twenty minutes of inserting the frozen marijuana butter rectally. It worked, without her feeling as stoned as the smoked marijuana.

My actions, though compassionate, were also illegal and if my medical school had found out I was acting as an apothecary, preparing an illicit drug for use for a non-FDA approved indication, I could have lost my student standing and future profession. I don't regret that I did what I could to help my friend when she needed it. Subsequent studies have confirmed the efficacy of marijuana, in various forms, for nausea from HIV and chemo, muscle spasm from multiple sclerosis and quadra- and paraplegia, some types of chronic pain, and glaucoma, yet it has never been seen by the medical community as a first line drug for any of those conditions. I have prescribed Marinol, the oral form of cannabis, in a few cases where it was warranted because of the refractory nature of the patient's symptoms, for indications that are supported by controlled clinical studies. This made sense and like most medications, it worked for some, not for all.

A Bit Too Common

Yet if you believe the extremely vocal marijuana proponents, cannabis can treat almost any condition under the sun, and in a number of states now is being prescribed and encouraged for everything from anxiety to insomnia to sinusitis to asthma to arthritis to headaches to premenstrual syndrome. If you are simply alive, there is a good chance you have at least one symptom that warrants a medical marijuana card. It is a fine example of a not so modern snake oil, as it has been around for thousands of years, except now we have multiple state legislative bodies putting their stamp of approval on it. I'm concerned our nation's overwhelming drug abuse statistics will not decline with the legalization of the possession of small amounts of marijuana for medicinal purposes, in addition to open marketing, sale and distribution. We are simply bringing the dealers and pushers out of the shadows—not a bad thing if we can all agree that a staggering percentage of the population, including our adolescents, suffer symptoms deemed worthy of being medicated with a mood altering substance well known to cause dependency, not to mention a host of psychiatric problems in vulnerable individuals.

Patients who have antipathy for the pharmaceutical industry or for government agencies responsible for studies of drug safety and effectiveness seem to lose their skepticism when confronting the for-profit motivation of marijuana growers, brokers and storefront sellers. These patients prefer to trust a physician willing to pocket $150 cash for a ten minute assessment of symptoms in exchange for a signature on a medical marijuana card. Many choose not to be followed by responsible health care providers who might actually take a thorough history, do a complete examination and lab tests including drugs of abuse testing, possibly order confirmatory imaging studies, and might actually recommend treatment that is proven in multiple controlled studies to be effective.

A Troubling Trend

Over the last few weeks in my university health center clinic I've been asked by several otherwise healthy teenage college students if I would prescribe medical marijuana for their stress-related daily headaches. These young people have friends who have gotten their medical marijuana card elsewhere so they can "smoke whenever they need to" without fear of being found in possession by law enforcement. They want the "get out of jail free" card, or better yet, "never get arrested to begin with" card. They have symptoms, as all of us do, but none of these are patients with chronic disease found unresponsive to other treatment. These are patients who have never had more than a cursory headache evaluation, never had a trial of non-pharmaceutical modalities like relaxation techniques or massage, or prophylaxis with non-addictive medication. Yet they are willing to sign on to a substance that has, at best, a shadowy origin, no quality standards in production, distribution or dosing, is traditionally and most expediently used only by inhaling, and has well-studied adverse effects on memory, focus and reaction time. All this defies logic, especially in a college student who needs every neuron at the ready to absorb, retain and process complex information, something marijuana has proven ability to impair. I'm perplexed at how easily these leaves of grass are given a pass by young and old, rich and poor, professional and blue collar, liberal and conservative.

Benumbed, Blunted, and Stunted

It could be that over twenty years of addiction treatment work with thousands of chemically dependent patients has warped my perspective about this weed forever. I see marijuana as the "least" of the problem recreational drugs, to be sure, and not nearly as physically devastating as alcohol, benzodiazepines, methamphetamines, or opiates. None the less, I've seen it ruin lives, not because of dangerous side effects, nor fatal overdoses, nor instigation of violent behavior. In its twenty first century ultra high concentrated version, far more powerful than the weed of the sixties and seventies, it just makes people so much less alive and engaged with the world. They are anesthetized to all the opportunities and challenges of life. You can see it in their eyes and hear it in their voices. In a young person who uses regularly, which a significant percentage choose to do in their fervent belief in its safety, it can mean more than temporary anesthesia to the unpleasantness of every day hassles. They never really experience life in its full emotional range from joy to sadness, learning the sensitivity of becoming vulnerable, the lessons of experiencing discomfort and coping, and the healing balm of a resilient spirit. Instead, it is all about avoidance.

Benumbed, blunted, and stunted. I'm sure this must be yet another indication for the prescription of medical marijuana.

Periodical and Internet Sources Bibliography

The following articles have been selected to supplement the diverse views presented in this chapter.

Peter Bensinger	"California Medical Marijuana Is a Public Danger," *US News & World Report*, October 26, 2011.
Nicole Brochu	"Teen Pot Smokers? Don't Blame Medical Marijuana Laws," *Sun Sentinel* (South FL), February 1, 2011.
Mitch Earleywine	"Medical Marijuana Benefits," CBS News, November 13, 2010. www.cbsnews.com
Kevin Fagan	"How Healthy—Or Dangerous—Is Marijuana Use?," *San Francisco Chronicle*, July 18, 2010. www.sfgate.com.
Charles V. Giannasio	"Marijuana Is Addictive, Destructive and Dangerous," CNBC, April 20, 2010. www.cnbc.com
Lucia Graves	"Marijuana, Narcotics Help Patients Reduce Chronic Pain, Study Finds," *Huffington Post*, December 8, 2011. www.huffingtonpost.com.
Natalie K. Munden	"My Medical Marijuana Story," *Salon*, January 1, 2010. www.salon.com.
Jodie Sinnema	"Painful Battle for Pot Was Worth the Fight," *Montreal Gazette*, December 9, 2011.
Maia Szalavitz	"US Rules That Marijuana Has No Medical Use. What Does Science Say?," *Time*, July 11, 2011.
Robert Townsend	"Show That Medical Marijuana Works," *Lansing State Journal*, December 10, 2011.

OPPOSING
VIEWPOINTS®
SERIES

CHAPTER  3

How Should Access to Medical Marijuana Be Managed?

Chapter Preface

In 2008 then-Senator Barack Obama was busy crossing the country campaigning to become the president of the United States. During his campaign speeches, he touched on the controversial subject of medical marijuana, clarifying his position on the federal role in policing state marijuana laws. Obama indicated that he did not have a problem with medical marijuana in states where it was legal. He pledged that as president he wouldn't devote federal law enforcement to prosecute growers, distributors, and medical marijuana users.

Initially, Obama kept his pledge. In 2009 he instructed the US Justice Department not to devote resources to "individuals whose actions are in clear and unambiguous compliance with existing state laws providing for the medical use of marijuana." In October 2009, David Ogden, a deputy attorney general, sent a memo indicating that the Justice Department would follow the president's stated position on the matter. As the Ogden memo directs: "As a general matter, pursuit of these priorities should not focus federal resources in your States on individuals whose actions are in clear and unambiguous compliance with existing state laws providing for the medical use of marijuana. . . . On the other hand, prosecution of commercial enterprises that unlawfully market and sell marijuana for profit continues to be an enforcement priority of the Department."

By 2010, however, it became clear that the Obama administration was not acting according to the Ogden memo. In a November 2011 op-ed in the *New York Times*, Ethan Nadelmann, the executive director of the Drug Policy Alliance, observed: "The Treasury Department has forced banks to close accounts of medical marijuana businesses operating legally under state law. The Internal Revenue Service has required dispensary owners to pay punitive taxes required of no other businesses. The Bureau of Alcohol, Tobacco, Firearms and Explosives recently ruled that state-sanctioned medical marijuana patients can not purchase firearms. United States attorneys have also sent letters to local officials, coinciding with the adoption or implementation of state medical marijuana regulatory legislation, stressing their authority to prosecute all marijuana offenses. Prosecutors have threatened to seize the property of landlords and put them behind bars for renting to marijuana dispensaries." For Nadelmann and other medical marijuana supporters, the actions of the Justice Department did not match Obama's clear directions on how to treat medical marijuana.

In June 2011 Deputy Attorney General James M. Cole put out a directive to clarify the Ogden memo. The Cole memo indicates that the Ogden memo never intended to shield the commercial cultivation, sale, distribution, and use of medical marijuana from criminal prosecution, even in states where medical marijuana is legal. The Cole memo states, "The Ogden Memorandum was never intended to shield such activities from federal enforcement action and prosecution, even where those activities purport to comply with state law. Persons who are in the business of cultivating, selling or distributing marijuana, and those who knowingly facilitate such activities, are in violation of the Controlled Substances Act, regardless of state law. Consistent with resource constraints and the discretion you may exercise in your district, such persons are subject to federal enforcement action, including potential prosecution."

The differing interpretations of the Ogden memo and the Obama administration's crackdown on medical marijuana are subjects examined in the following chapter, which explores how access to medical marijuana should be managed.

> *"Medical marijuana laws in states such as New Mexico, and last week in New Jersey, include safeguards to ensure the drug is prescribed for a true medical need."*

Medical Marijuana Dispensaries Need More Regulation

Tristan Scott

Tristan Scott is a reporter for The Missoulian. *In the following viewpoint, he reports that Montana legislators are likely to amend the state's medical marijuana law with an eye toward more effective regulations for marijuana dispensaries. Proposals to reform the law, Scott explains, aim to prevent fraud and exploitation by enhancing oversight of caregivers who can legally provide medical marijuana to patients through a comprehensive tracking system. Another goal, Scott adds, is to limit the number of licensed dispensaries. Scott contends that many lawmakers are looking to the example of California, where lax oversight and regulations have caused intense controversy, for what not to do.*

As you read, consider the following questions:

1. According to Scott, how many registered caregivers are there in Montana who can legally provide medical marijuana to patients?
2. How does Missoula County Attorney Fred Van Valkenburg view the concept of licensed caregivers, according to Scott?
3. According to Scott, how many state medical marijuana laws have been amended at least once?

Proposed regulations to reshape Montana's medical marijuana law are likely to crop up next legislative session, with special consideration on how to govern the rising number of marijuana dispensaries.

Improving Patient Care

Medical marijuana advocates, licensed pot growers, lawmakers and law enforcement officials say tighter regulations could improve care to patients the incipient law is meant to serve, while preventing profiteers from exploiting and undermining the law.

"I certainly expect there to be a lot of legislative debate this next year about the medical marijuana law, and I expect to make some proposals myself for improving the law," said Tom Daubert, the president of Patients and Families United who helped craft the 2004 Medical Marijuana Act. "Some of my proposals address the same concerns that law enforcement have. When you get down to it, there is more common ground between law enforcement and patients than you might imagine."

Key Issues

A key issue will be better oversight of the nearly 2,000 registered caregivers who can legally provide medical marijuana to patients. Recently, some of those caregivers have opened medical marijuana dispensaries out of their homes, as well as storefront operations that cater to hundreds of patients.

The dispensaries have risen to the fore since last October [2009], when the Obama administration announced it would not interfere with states' medical marijuana laws. In the 14 states with medical marijuana laws, the announcement has been a watershed event, emboldening growers to advertise and promote their services.

Requiring Accountability

Daubert says new legislation requiring caregivers to document the quantity of marijuana they produce and show where it is distributed would lend more accountability to what's become a legal gray area.

"There needs to be a better means of accountability, and there needs to be a tracking system to show that 100 percent of what is grown goes to patients with legitimate needs," Daubert said. "I would expect that some of the people trying to profit right now, people who are exploitative of the law, would not bother under those circumstances. I think good regulation would flush that kind of thing out. After all, the point of this isn't profiteering, it's patient service."

Limiting the Growth of the Industry

Missoula County Attorney Fred Van Valkenburg said the Montana Legislature has a responsibility to take a hard look at the Medical Marijuana Act, which was born of a voter-approved initiative. Dispensaries in particular need to be regulated, he said, to ensure they don't expand boundlessly.

"I hope to see (the dispensaries) reigned in quite a bit because it just seems like the whole business of medical marijuana has gotten out of control, in Montana and elsewhere," Van Valkenburg said. "People have been able to expand their operations tremendously. I don't think we should do away with dispensaries altogether, but this has become a big-time business,

What Are Medical Marijuana Dispensaries?

Medical marijuana dispensaries are storefront locations where patients and caregivers with a doctor's prescription are allowed to obtain their medication, without the fear of repercussion or prosecution of the law. Many of these medical marijuana dispensaries have a variety of cannabis, from smoking the medical marijuana to consumables like candy bars, cakes, cookies, beverages, ice cream, and even hot sauce. With one location that provides all your needs, many medical marijuana patients prefer this method of obtaining their medication, as opposed to illegally obtaining their medication from an unknown, dangerous source.

Source: "Medical Marijuana Dispensary."
www.medicalmarijuanadispensary.net, 2011.

and that is not what I think was ever intended by the caregiver provision of the Medical Marijuana Act. If somebody is an actual caregiver, they really ought to have a relatively limited number of people they are providing marijuana for, in the ballpark of five patients. These people think the law allows them an unlimited number, and they just become a retail operation."

The Concept of Caregivers

Van Valkenburg said the idea behind licensed "caregivers" when the Medical Marijuana Act was first proposed was to benefit patients who were unable to cultivate the drug without assistance; it was not intended as a business model.

"I think the idea of a caregiver when this was initially passed was to help people who were in the throes of death, people with cancer who were desperate for some kind of pain relief who could not grow marijuana themselves," Van Valkenburg said. "It wasn't meant to sanction clinics that OK someone because they have a headache, or some other condition that technically meets the letter of the law."

The spike in the number of people who have applied to be patients and caregivers in recent months is a good indication that additional legislation is needed, he said.

Amending the Law

In the 14 states with medical marijuana laws on the books, six laws have been amended at least once, and proposals to Montana and Washington law will likely emerge in 2011.

Alison Holcomb, drug policy director for the American Civil Liberties Union in Washington state, says she hopes the new legislation will focus on safeguarding the rights of patients with a legitimate need for medical marijuana.

Holcomb would like to see dispensaries in Washington regulated in a way that ensures patients who can benefit from medical marijuana have access to it, while avoiding the shortcomings of state laws like California's, whose provisions are viewed by some as lax and subject to abuse. Dispensaries in California are not subject to any regulation.

"We want to avoid the political backlash that has occurred in the wake of what's happening in California," Holcomb said. "We don't want to see public support of medical marijuana diminish because the law is being abused by profiteers."

Learning from California's Mistakes

Medical marijuana laws in states such as New Mexico, and last week in New Jersey, include safeguards to ensure the drug is prescribed for a true medical need and have highly regulated systems for licensing dispensaries and monitoring their operations.

"The laws are recent enough that we haven't had a lot of time to see how well they play out on the ground, but I suspect it's going to be a very different experience than what we've seen in California where there are no rules for how a dispensary is supposed to operate," Holcomb said.

Derek Deese is a medical marijuana caregiver in Missoula with about eight active patients. He worries that too many providers are operating carte blanche, with an emphasis on profits rather than on following the law. That could have a negative impact on providers who want to be legitimate, he said.

"Some people are using this as a front. They're using it as a cover to still deal drugs," Deese said. "There's so many gray areas in the law right now that it's really wide open. It's being interpreted like a set of tarot cards. People are interpreting it and twisting it to their own advantage.

"They need to make stricter guidelines," Deese said.

More Regulation Is Necessary

Tom Berry, a Republican state lawmaker whose son was killed by a drug dealer in 2000, says he's not altogether opposed to medical marijuana, but intends to carry bills next session to create more rigorous oversight of caregivers, and implement guidelines for licensing marijuana dispensaries.

"After observing the situation with the caretakers these past several months, I will look at imposing more regulations on how they produce and distribute the medical marijuana," Berry said. "The way it stands, it appears we have more restrictions for beer and wine licenses than we have for opening a marijuana dispensary."

"Such restrictions reflect marijuana's dual identity in California: It is simultaneously medicine and menace."

Excessive Regulation of Medical Marijuana Dispensaries Is Discriminatory

Brian Doherty

Brian Doherty is an author and senior editor at Reason. *In the following viewpoint, he suggests that the stringent regulations on marijuana dispensaries passed by the Los Angeles city council are discriminatory and reveal US culture's inconsistent attitude toward the drug. Much of the push behind tighter regulations, Doherty argues, comes from neighborhood activists worried about blight and increased crime in areas with dispensaries or officials worried about patients gaming the system to get legal access to marijuana. Some activists, the author explains, are also worried that the visibility and widespread acceptance of medical marijuana in mainstream US culture will lead to full legalization.*

As you read, consider the following questions:

1. According to Doherty, how many marijuana dispensaries are there in Los Angeles?
2. According to an October 2009 poll of Los Angeles residents cited in the viewpoint, what percentage supported regulating marijuana dispensaries?
3. What percent of the people entering Los Angeles area marijuana dispensaries were "young men," according to a report by the *LA Weekly* cited by Doherty?

On a warm, bright winter day in January [2010], I spent a few hours driving around two neighborhoods in Los Angeles, looking at marijuana stores.

You know, marijuana stores. Where you (well, not necessarily *you*) can walk in and, if you can prove a doctor has recommended marijuana to you for relief of an ailment, walk out with a brown bag full of buds, pot brownies, or cannabis candy bars. Los Angeles has more than 500 of these stores. My companions on the drives were two citizen activists who didn't like seeing so many marijuana shops and who regularly let the Los Angeles City Council know of their unhappiness.

Michael Larsen, a 43-year-old family man, is public safety director for the Eagle Rock Neighborhood Council. He doesn't like to discuss his day job in the press, saying it has drawn too many hostile medical marijuana supporters to his work-related websites in the past.

Eagle Rock

Eagle Rock, a neighborhood in northeast Los Angeles, is visibly aging but remains dignified and distinct, with commercial areas occupied mostly by low-slung, pale old buildings housing storefront doctor's offices, service businesses such as beauty salons and tax preparers, and independent restaurants and boutiques rather than chain stores. As we cruise a mile or so up and down Eagle

Rock, York, and Colorado boulevards, Larsen points out more than 10 pot dispensaries. "Eagle Rock is about being a small community with a small-town feel, and we want to retain that," he says.

Responding to criticisms he's received from medical marijuana activists, Larsen insists: "I'm not being uncompassionate. I may be a NIMBY [Not in My Back Yard], but I'm fine with that. Eagle Rock is struggling to maintain the character of the neighborhood, for my kids or other people and their kids." Larsen tells me about the healthy-looking young men who sometimes congregate in parking lots or on streets near dispensaries, smoking pot or blasting music. He points out one such young man entering AEC, a dispensary on Colorado Boulevard, while we are in its parking lot. He tells me about a local woman in her 80s who can't understand what kind of world she's living in, where marijuana is sold on her corner.

Larsen also points out some grubby-looking auto repair shops along his neighborhood's main strip and tells me how the locals managed to curb their profusion through the city's planning process. He talks about the auto repair shops in much the same way he discusses the pot shops. He does not think either should be completely eliminated, but he believes they constitute a blight on the neighborhood when they are too conspicuous.

Larsen and I pass one marijuana dispensary, the Cornerstone Collective, that I visited the day before. If you didn't know it was there, you wouldn't know it was there. It has no pot leaf images, no neon signs announcing "Alternative" or "Herbal," no commercial signage at all. The owner, Michael Backes, told me with amused pride that a while back, when a runaway car plowed straight through his wall, a local news crew identified the place as a "dentist office," which is what it looks like from its waiting room. Backes is "doing it right," Larsen tells me.

Studio City

My drive through Studio City, in the southeast San Fernando Valley just over the mountains from Hollywood, is similar.

Barbara Monahan Burke, a 64-year-old horticulturalist who serves as the neighborhood council's co-chair for government affairs, doesn't say anything about increases in crime associated with the marijuana dispensaries (a connection often asserted by public officials), but she does complain about occasional pot smoking in front of them, which can annoy commercial neighbors. "I personally believe in compassionate use of medical marijuana and voted for it," she says.

Within a couple of miles on Ventura Boulevard, a dozen dispensaries seem to be open for business on this weekday afternoon. (Burke told me in mid-February that by then she was only sure that six of them were still open for business.) "It's about preservation of communities," she says. "We want this to be a place where families can live. It's about, what do the people who live here want our branding to be as Studio City?" That branding, she thinks, should not be linked to green crosses and billboards for Medicann, a medical marijuana doctors' consulting service, every couple of blocks on her neighborhood's major commercial strip.

The Wild West of Weed

Newsweek dubbed Los Angeles "the wild West of weed" in October 2009, and that phrase often echoed through the city council's chamber as it haggled over a long-awaited ordinance regulating the dispensaries. Both the *Los Angeles Times* and the *L.A. Weekly* regularly jabbed at the city council for fiddling while marijuana burned, supplied by storefront pot dispensaries that were widely (but inaccurately) said to total 1,000 or more.

On January 26 [2010], after years of dithering and months of debate, the city council finally passed an ordinance to regulate medical marijuana shops. In addition to dictating the details of lighting, record keeping, auditing, bank drops, hours of operation, and compensation for owners and employees, the ordinance requires a dramatic reduction in the number of dispensaries. The official limit is 70, but because of exemptions for some pre-existing dispensaries the final number could grow as high as 137. The ordinance allocates the surviving dispensaries among the city's "planning districts" and requires that they be located more than 1,000 feet from each other and from "sensitive areas" such as parks, schools, churches, and libraries. It also requires patients who obtain marijuana from dispensaries to pick one outlet and stick with it.

Discriminatory Policies

As those rules suggest, city officials are not prepared to treat marijuana like any other medicine, despite a 1996 state ballot initiative that allows patients with doctor's recommendations to use it for symptom relief. It's hard to imagine the city council arbitrarily limiting the number of pharmacies, insisting that they not do business near competitors, creating buffer zones between parks and Duane Reade locations, or demanding that patients obtain their Lipitor from one and only one drugstore. Such restrictions reflect marijuana's dual identity in California: It is simultaneously medicine and menace. At the same time, the regulations do serve to legitimize distribution of a drug that remains completely prohibited by federal law—a stamp of approval welcomed by many dispensary operators.

When I asked activists, businessmen, or politicians why L.A.'s medical marijuana market needed to be regulated, they almost invariably replied, "It was unregulated." When I delved beyond that tautology, I found motives little different from those that drive land use planning generally. The activists who demanded that the city bring order to the "wild West" of medical marijuana were motivated not by antipathy to cannabis so much as mundane concerns about "blight," neighborhood character, and spillover effects. While responding to these concerns, every member of the city council voiced support for medical access to marijuana in theory, and none openly sided with the federal law enforcement officials who view the trade as nothing more than drug dealing in disguise.

The L.A. Experience with Marijuana Dispensaries

Los Angeles became the medical marijuana capital of America thanks to a combination of entrepreneurial energy and benign political neglect. What happened here is instructive for other jurisdictions that already or may soon let patients use the drug. In the last 14 years, the voters or legislators of 14 states and the District of Columbia have legalized marijuana for at least some medical purposes. Medical marijuana campaigns, via either legislation or ballot initiative, are active in 13 other states. National surveys indicate broad public support for such reforms. An ABC News/*Washington Post* poll conducted in January found that 81 percent of Americans think patients who can benefit from marijuana should be able to obtain it legally.

But L.A.'s experience also shows that majority support for medical marijuana is not necessarily enough. An October poll of Los Angeles residents commissioned by the Marijuana Policy Project found that 77 percent supported regulating dispensaries, while only 14 percent wanted them closed. But patients and the entrepreneurs who served them still had to contend with a noisy minority, clustered in political institutions such as neighborhood councils, the police department, and government lawyers' offices, who resisted the normalization of marijuana. That process culminated in an ordinance with onerous restrictions that could nearly eliminate the current medical pot business and cause great hardship for tens of thousands of Los Angeles residents who use marijuana as a medicine.

Still, for those who lived through the ferocious cultural and political war over pot during the second half of the 20th century, it's amazing that the strife in pot-saturated Los Angeles has had more to do with land use regulation than with eradicating an allegedly evil plant. Even with pot readily available over the counter at hundreds of locations to anyone with an easily obtained doctor's letter, the most common complaints were essentially aesthetic. . . .

The Lie of Medical Marijuana

California's medical marijuana law created a special category of people who are allowed to do something that others would be arrested for doing, and it gave a guild of licensed professionals the nearly unlimited power to define this category. Although physicians who issue recommendations for nonmedical reasons theoretically can be disciplined by the state medical board, that has happened only 12 times since 1996, and only one doctor lost his license as a result. The discretion permitted by the law is so broad that proving misconduct is very difficult.

That broad discretion helps patients who might be denied their medicine under a stricter regime, and at the same time it helps people who want pot for recreational purposes. Medical marijuana activists often say that *all* marijuana use is essentially medical, if that category is understood to include quotidian psychological and emotional problems that the drug alleviates. If physicians can prescribe pharmaceuticals to treat stress, anxiety, shyness, and depression, the activists say, why can't they recommend marijuana for the same reasons? Stephen Gutwillig, California state director of the Drug Policy Alliance, offers a partly tongue-in-cheek take on the question: Given how bad for your health it is to get caught up in the criminal justice system because you have marijuana, he says, removing that threat is a form of preventive medicine.

Politically, though, the malleability of the medical category is a problem. Anyone who locates a sympathetic, trusting, or simply greedy doctor can obtain the legal right to possess pot in California. That fact, plus the hundreds of outlets that sprang up in Los Angeles to supply those patients, fostered a fairly accurate public perception that during the last few years anyone willing to put in a little effort could travel a short distance and buy pot over the counter.

The Right Reasons

The medical model attaches great importance to motive and state of mind, which is why dispensary operators often say, when justifying themselves to politicians or the press, that they're in the business "for the right reasons," unlike some of their competitors. Combined with the federal ban on marijuana, medicalization leads to a world where customers can shop at only one store; where the cash they pay for a product is not the price but a "contribution to the collective"; where businesses are expected to avoid turning a profit; where a medicine is subject to sales tax, unlike other pharmaceuticals, and isn't regulated like any other pharmaceutical; where you are complying with the law if what you possess is "reasonable" related to some need that may have been invented by a doctor to begin with; where it's legal for you to have pot but you are still apt to be arrested for growing or transporting it.

The medical model also fosters a weirdly contradictory attitude toward pot use, one that seemed to animate the *L.A. Weekly*'s surprisingly negative coverage of the issue: Even people who don't care about pot smoking in general get upset when they think stoners are gaming a system that is supposed to serve patients with doctor-certified needs. The *L.A. Weekly* angrily reported in November that 70 percent of the people its reporters saw entering dispensaries were "young men—corroborating D.A. Cooley's claim that the real market for all this activity is everyday users, not people suffering serious disease." (Medical activists tend to respond to that sort of talk with the riposte that all sorts of maladies for which pot provides relief aren't diagnosable by strangers watching from yards away.)

The Wrong Reasons

In Los Angeles, such outrage over pot being used for the "wrong" reasons led to a bad and unsustainable ordinance. In March, Americans for Safe Access challenged the new regulations in state court. Its lawyer Joe Elford said in a press release that "The requirement to find a new location within 7 days [if the old one is zoned out of compliance] is completely unreasonable and undermines the due process of otherwise legal medical marijuana dispensaries." The suit seeks to have the ordinance declared "unlawful and unconstitutional."

The ordinance also faces a challenge in the form of a citizen referendum spearheaded by Dan Halbert, who needs 27,000 signatures to get it on the next available L.A. ballot in 2010. But as long as medical use is the only marijuana use officially permitted, dispensaries will remain hamstrung by stupid and unworkable restrictions. Full legalization, an idea long avoided by many medical marijuana activists, may be the only way to make sure all patients who can benefit from the drug have access to it without creating the sort of situation that gave rise to the crackdown in L.A.

The Pot Culture

While the latest ordinance may or may not succeed in shutting down hundreds of functioning storefronts, the freewheeling culture of quasi-legal pot will be harder to crush. L.A. is home to at least four ad-filled magazines serving the pot community, a branch of "Oaksterdam University" where potrepreneurs and patients learn medical marijuana science and law, an endless series of cannabis-related expositions and conventions, and websites such as Weedtracker (featuring discussions of dispensary quality and local politics) and weedmaps.com (which finds the dispensary nearest you). The Medical Cannabis Safety Council meets at Oaksterdam on occasional Saturday nights to discuss, among other things, the molds that can bedevil growers and self-regulation as a way of fending off heavy-handed government interference.

Is America ready for a world in which pot is as culturally and physically prevalent as it has become in L.A.? In a national Zogby poll conducted in April 2009, 52 percent of respondents supported treating marijuana more or less like alcohol, while other recent polls put the percentage in the 40s. Support for legalization is higher in California: A Field Poll of California voters taken the same month as the Zogby survey put support for legalization at 56 percent statewide and 60 percent in Los Angeles

How Should Access to Medical Marijuana Be Managed?

County. This fall we will see whether those opinions translate into voter support for a California ballot initiative that would, at long last, legalize and tax adult possession of marijuana.

Full Legalization

Don Duncan, as dean of L.A.'s medical marijuana suppliers and activists, doesn't want to opine about full legalization. But his take on why all sides have fought so ferociously over the city's medical pot ordinance applies to the legalization debate as well. "The normalization of medical marijuana—certain elements in law enforcement and other civic leaders see it as a threat," he says. "If L.A. is in fact a medical marijuana town with safe access regulated, then that ends the debate for California. . . . Once the state's largest and most populated community has sensible regulations, foes of medical cannabis in law enforcement know they've lost the battle in California. They see it as a line in the sand, so ideologically they can't give up L.A. By the same token, that's why ideologically we can't either."

The fight to define what happened in L.A. during the "wild West" days of what amounted to legal over-the-counter pot is the same sort of battle. If the complaints that led to the regulatory crackdown are understood as arising from anti-pot prejudice, NIMBYism [the conviction that such activity should occur "Not in My Back Yard"], and the occasional sighting of "undesirables," rather than real threats to public order and safety, it will seem pretty silly to continue spending billions of dollars and millions of man-hours each year to stop people from exchanging money for pot. The accidental result of a city attorney who didn't want to legitimize marijuana and a city council that didn't want to think about it could be the realization that it's better to allow a pot free-for-all than to continue to wage war on marijuana.

> "States could take the new policy as a tacit nod from Uncle Sam to go ahead and allow medical marijuana back home."

The Ogden Memo Will Relax Medical Marijuana Enforcement

Christopher Beam

Christopher Beam is a reporter for Slate. *In the following viewpoint, he speculates that the Ogden memo, a federal government directive to district attorneys that urges them to defer to local marijuana laws rather than federal law, will have a profound effect on both states in which medical marijuana is legal and in which it is not. In the former case, Beam contends that the Ogden memo will mean fewer crackdowns on legal marijuana dispensaries. In the latter, he argues that the Ogden memo will lead to more states legalizing medical marijuana.*

As you read, consider the following questions:

1. According to Beam, what percentage of Americans think marijuana should be legal for medicinal purposes?

Christopher Beam, "Gateway Drug Policy," *Slate.com*, October 19, 2009. Copyright © 2009 by Slate.com. All rights reserved. Reproduced by permission.

2. How many dispensaries does the author say have sprouted up in Los Angeles County since 2002?
3. What did the Controlled Substances Act aim to do, according to the viewpoint?

W ill [President Barack] Obama's new medical marijuana directive actually change anything?

The Justice Department's announcement that the feds will no longer crack down on medical marijuana sellers who follow state laws will surely cheer the liberal/libertarian axis that wants the government to take a more relaxed stance on drug laws. It should also please conservatives who champion states' rights as the highest political ideal. But unlike most policies with such broad support, it might actually accomplish something.

The Ogden Memo

The new memo, written by Deputy Attorney General David Ogden, urges district attorneys to defer to local marijuana laws rather than federal law, which prohibits all consumption and sales of the drug. The new policy is remarkably uncontroversial. Two-thirds of Americans think marijuana should be legal for medicinal purposes. Obama promised during his campaign to reduce crackdowns on dispensaries; opposition was minimal. Attorney General Eric Holder said in March that the crackdowns would stop and met with little objection. Monday's memo simply made it official. "This is a very safe policy," says Bruce Mirken of the Marijuana Policy Project. "There's no constituency for going after sick people."

On the one hand, the decision to defer to state laws means that existing local drug policies—however strict or lax—will remain in place. But on the other, many states take their cues from the federal government when it comes to drug policy. States could take the new policy as a tacit nod from Uncle Sam to go ahead and allow medical marijuana back home.

An Excerpt from the Ogden Memo

The prosecution of significant traffickers of illegal drugs, including marijuana, and the disruption of illegal drug manufacturing and trafficking networks continues to be a core priority in the Department's efforts against narcotics and dangerous drugs, and the Department's investigative and prosecutorial resources should be directed towards these objectives. As a general matter, pursuit of these priorities should not focus federal resources in your States on individuals whose actions are in clear and unambiguous compliance with existing state laws providing for the medical use of marijuana. For example, prosecution of individuals with cancer or other serious illnesses who use marijuana as part of a recommended treatment regimen consistent with applicable state law, or those caregivers in clear and unambiguous compliance with existing state law who provide such individuals with marijuana, is unlikely to be an efficient use of limited federal resources. On the other hand, prosecution of commercial enterprises that unlawfully market and sell marijuana for profit continues to be an enforcement priority of the Department. To be sure, claims of compliance with state or local law may mask operations inconsistent with the terms, conditions, or purposes of those laws, and federal law enforcement should not be deterred by such assertions when otherwise pursuing the Department's core enforcement priorities.

Source: David Ogden, "Memorandum for Selected US Attorneys on Investigations and Prosecutions in States Authorizing the Medical Use of Marijuana," US Department of Justice, October 19, 2009.

The Case of California

Take California. It has long experience with medical marijuana—voters approved the drug for sick people back in 1996—yet in many ways the state stands as a cautionary tale of what not to do. The main problem is that the California law is vaguely worded: It says patients can use marijuana for medical purposes, they can grow it, and they can buy it. But it doesn't specifically authorize anyone to start a pot business. The law's vagueness has led to roughly 1,000 dispensaries sprouting up in Los Angeles County since 2002. Now local law-enforcement officials are promising to bust them up, arguing that the law allows only nonprofit businesses.

Ogden's new memo won't change that. If you run a medical marijuana business in Los Angeles that the state deems illegal, the federal government can't help you. In fact, it can still raid your facility. The only dispensaries that will benefit directly from the new federal policy are those that were raided by the DEA under the Bush administration despite complying with California statutes. (President Bush claimed they violated the Controlled Substances Act, which prohibits the growing and consumption of marijuana.) But if California courts agree with the Los Angeles County district attorney that "about 100 percent of dispensaries in Los Angeles County and the city are operating illegally," those vendors are out of luck.

Taking the Cue from Federal Drug Policy

Where the new federal guidelines could have an effect is on states currently considering medical marijuana laws. Right now, 13 states allow some degree of medical marijuana consumption. (There are 14 if you count Maryland, which reduces the penalty if the marijuana you're caught using is for medical purposes.) Another dozen or so have bills moving through their legislature. In many cases, lawmakers have been skittish about OKing dispensaries for fear that the Drug Enforcement Administration would come and shut them down. Now that's no longer a concern. The memo also changes the way the federal government treats marijuana vendors in states that already allow medical marijuana. The drug is technically legal for medical purposes in New Mexico, but the only person with a license to sell it has refused reveal her identity for fear of federal punishment. Without that looming threat, the number of dispensaries is likely to increase.

Most states take their cues from the federal government on drug policy. The practice traces back to passage of the Controlled Substances Act of 1970, which aimed to create a uniform set of drug regulations across the country. During the drug war in the 1980s and '90s, the federal government started awarding grants to help states with law enforcement in exchange for aligning their drug policies with federal guidelines. So when the federal government signals its preference not to pursue medical marijuana users, states may take the cue.

A Growing Trend Toward Legalization

First in line is probably New Jersey. Gov. Jon Corzine has said that if a medical marijuana bill landed on his desk, he'd sign it. In a recent debate, his two electoral opponents made the same promise. The state's Democratic leadership now expects a bill to pass the legislature some time in late November. "We're already getting calls from people in Atlantic City buying store fronts," says Allen St. Pierre of the National Organization for the Reform of Marijuana Laws. Massachusetts voters could approve a similar bill as soon as 2010, and Gov. Deval Patrick seems inclined to sign it. New York Gov. David Paterson would probably sign a medical marijuana bill, but the chaotic state legislature seems unlikely to produce one. Massachusetts and New York and Ohio have already decriminalized marijuana but haven't gotten around to legalizing medicinal marijuana consumption. The popular will is there—it's just a matter of time.

In his memo, Ogden stresses that this is not a small step on the slippery slope toward legalization: "This guidance regarding resource allocation does not 'legalize' marijuana or provide a legal defense to a violation of federal law." But the memo is still a strong symbolic deprioritization of low-level marijuana enforcement. Given limited resources, it says, we should focus on serious drug traffickers rather than small-time consumers.

The law also sets a precedent for leaving hot-button issues to the states. No one is saying—not yet, anyway—that if the federal government believes it should defer to the states on marijuana laws, then it should also defer to the states on, say, marriage laws. But the argument wouldn't be that much of a stretch. It's just ironic that the debate would take place under a liberal Democratic president.

| "The Ogden memo was never the panacea the media trumpeted it to be."

The Ogden Memo Did Not Change Federal Medical Marijuana Enforcement Policies

Jeralyn E. Merritt

Jeralyn E. Merritt is an attorney and blogger. In the following viewpoint, she analyzes a 2011 Department of Justice memo that aims to clarify the 2009 Ogden memo, which indicated that federal resources should not be used to prosecute those following state medical marijuana laws. Merritt finds that the Ogden memo did not substantially change federal policy on medical marijuana. She notes that federal marijuana policy is essentially the same as it was under presidents Bill Clinton, Ronald Reagan, and Richard Nixon.

As you read, consider the following questions:

1. How does the Department of Justice describe its attitude toward enforcement of the Controlled Substances Act (CSA), according to Merritt?

2. Who licenses commercial enterprises to grow marijuana for medical marijuana patients, according to the viewpoint?

3. According to Merritt, how old is the War on Drugs?

The Department of Justice issued a new memo to federal prosecutors yesterday [June 29, 2011] further "clarifying" its 2009 Ogden Memorandum. The Odgen memorandum said federal resources should not be used to prosecute those in "clear and unambiguous" compliance with state medical marijuana laws.

Clarifying the Ogden Memo

Sorry, the new memo says, that's not what we meant. We only meant federal resources shouldn't be used to prosecute cancer patients and other seriously ill people who used marijuana in compliance with state law. We never meant to provide a shield for those who supply medical marijuana to those in full compliance with state law.

> The Ogden Memorandum was never intended to shield such activities from federal enforcement action and prosecution, even where those activities purport to comply with state law. Persons who are in the business of cultivating, selling or dis tributing marijuana, and those who knowingly facilitate such activities, are in violation of the Controlled Substances Act [CSA], regardless of state law. Consistent with resource constraints and the discretion you may exercise in your district, such persons are subject to federal enforcement action, including potential prosecution. State laws or local ordinances are not a defense to civil or criminal enforcement of federal law with respect to such conduct, including enforcement of the CSA. Those who engage in transactions involving the proceeds of such activity may also be in violation of federal money laundering statutes and other federal financial laws.

The Department of Justice is tasked with enforcing existing federal criminal laws in all states, and enforcement of the CSA has long been and remains a core priority.

Where did the Ogden memo exclude medical marijuana growers operating in compliance with state law? It said:

As a general matter, pursuit of these priorities should not focus federal resources in your States on individuals whose actions are in clear and unambiguous compliance with existing state laws providing for the medical use of marijuana. For example, prosecution of individuals with cancer or other serious illnesses who use marijuana as part of a recommended treatment regimen consistent with applicable state law, or those caregivers in clear and unambiguous compliance with existing state law who provide such individuals with marijuana, is unlikely to be an efficient use of limited federal resources. On the other hand, prosecution of commercial enterprises that *unlawfully* market and sell marijuana for profit continues to be an enforcement priority of the Department. (my emphasis)

Since all marijuana cultivation, marketing and sale is unlawful under federal law, the word "unlawful" in the last sentence is superfluous unless it is referring to state law. If they didn't mean it to refer to state law, the sentence would have read:

On the other hand, prosecution of commercial enterprises that market and sell marijuana for profit continues to be an enforcement priority of the Department.

Ogden Memo and State Laws

States are licensing commercial enterprises to grow marijuana for medical marijuana patients. If in compliance with state law, they are not operating illegally in that state. Under the Ogden

An Excerpt from the Cole Memo
Clarifying the Ogden Memo

A number of states have enacted some form of legislation relating to the medical use of marijuana. Accordingly the Ogden memo reiterated to you that prosecution of significant traffickers in illegal drugs, including marijuana, remains a core priority, but advised that it is likely not an efficient use of federal resources to focus enforcement efforts on individuals with cancer or other serious illnesses who use marijuana as part of a recommended treatment regimen consistent with applicable state law, or their caregivers. The term "caregiver" as used in the memorandum meant just that: individuals providing care to individuals with cancer or other serious illnesses, not commercial operations cultivating, selling or distributing marijuana.

The Department's view of the efficient use of limited federal resources as articulated in the Ogden Memorandum has not changed.

Source: James M. Cole, "Guidance
Regarding the Ogden Memo in Jurisdictions
Seeking to Authorize Marijuana for Medical
Use," US Department of Justice, June 29, 2011.

memo, they were covered. Further indication the Odgen memo never meant to bar commercial enterprises operating in compliance with state law: The next sentence reads:

To be sure, claims of compliance with state or local law *may mask* operations inconsistent with the terms, conditions, or purposes of those laws, and federal law enforcement should not be deterred by such assertions when otherwise pursuing the Department's core enforcement priorities. (my emphasis)

It didn't say:

Compliance with state or local law is inconsistent with federal law and federal law enforcement should not be deterred by such compliance when pursuing the Department's core enforcement priorities.

Which is what yesterday's memo clearly says. Also note the "clarification" in yesterday's memo to the definition of "caregiver."

The term "caregiver" as used in the memorandum meant just that: individuals providing care to individuals with cancer or other serious illnesses, not commercial operations cultivating, selling or distributing marijuana.

That's not what the Ogden memo said. It said:

As a general matter, pursuit of these priorities should not focus federal resources in your States on individuals whose actions are in clear and unambiguous compliance with existing state laws providing for the medical use of marijuana. *For example*, prosecution of individuals with cancer or other serious illnesses who use marijuana as part of a recommended treatment regimen consistent with applicable state law, *or those caregivers in clear and unambiguous compliance with existing state law who provide such individuals with marijuana*, is unlikely to be an efficient use of limited federal resources. On the other hand, prosecution of commercial enterprises that *unlawfully* market and sell marijuana for profit continues to be an enforcement priority of the Department. (my emphasis)

State laws allowing medical marijuana use allow caregivers to grow and provide marijuana to patients. The Ogden memo said caregivers who provide marijuana to patients in compliance with state law are an example of those against whom federal law enforcement resources should not be directed. Only unlawful commercial enterprises were excluded.

Bait and Switch

This is not a clarification, it's a bait and switch. Of course, the Ogden memo was never the panacea the media trumpeted it to be. It ended with:

> Indeed, this memorandum does not alter in any way the Department's authority to enforce federal law, including laws prohibiting the manufacture, production, distribution, possession, or use of marijuana on federal property. This guidance regarding resource allocation does not "legalize" marijuana or provide a legal defense to a violation of federal law, nor is it intended to create any privileges, benefits, or rights, substantive or procedural, enforceable by any individual, party or witness in any administrative, civil, or criminal matter.
>
> Nor does clear and unambiguous compliance with state law or the absence of one or all of the above factors create a legal defense to a violation of the Controlled Substances Act. Rather, this memorandum is intended solely as a guide to the exercise of investigative and prosecutorial discretion.

What a worthless guide it turned out to be. Shorter version: Federal marijuana policy today is the same as it ever was, under Bush, Clinton, Reagan and Nixon. In this, the 40th year of the war on drugs, the only sure thing is there will be a 41st year.

"It seems quite plausible that marijuana could be scientifically shown to bring a sense of calmness and pleasantness into a life burdened with harsh combat memories."

Veterans Should Have Access to Medical Marijuana to Treat Post-Traumatic Stress Disorder

John Grant

John Grant is a writer and photographer. In the following viewpoint, he underscores the need for serious research on the beneficial effects of marijuana for the symptoms of post-traumatic stress disorder (PTSD). Grant relates the stories of several veterans who found relief from their PTSD symptoms through the use of marijuana and contends that the cultural stigma and legal ramifications of marijuana use has hindered its application as an efficacious medicine for conditions like PTSD. He argues that although marijuana has some admittedly subversive qualities, veterans might need that subversiveness in order to deal with mental and emotional anguish.

As you read, consider the following questions:

1. In the proposed study discussed by Grant, how many combat veterans does Doblin want to study?
2. According to Sigmund Freud, cited by Grant, what is the greatest impediment to civilization?
3. What is the Greek term sometimes used for the death instinct, according to Grant?

Every once in a while a news story pops up that initially makes you want to laugh because it brings to mind an absurdity of modern life. In this case, the absurdity involves two major national issues: Helping war-stressed combat veterans cope with life back home and the 40-year-old War On Drugs.

Allowing Research to Go Forward

The *New York Times* reported recently that a group of researchers want to launch a study on the benefits of marijuana for Iraq and Afghanistan combat veterans who suffer Post Traumatic Stress Disorder (PTSD). The question looming over the study is will a stubborn federal government mired in the Drug War allow the study to even get off the ground.

The *Times* reports on an Iraq veteran in Texas suffering from a leg wound and several head injuries who told them "marijuana helped quiet his physical and psychological pain, while not causing weight loss and sleep deprivation brought on by his prescription medications." It seems "the munchies" can be beneficial to someone facing loss of appetite and emaciation.

"'I have seen it with my own eyes,' he said. 'It works for a lot of the guys coming home.'"

The Benefits of Marijuana for Veterans

I know a number of Vietnam and Iraq veterans who use marijuana. From my very unscientific survey it seems quite plausible that marijuana could be scientifically shown to bring a sense of calmness and pleasantness into a life burdened with harsh combat memories.

One vet who uses it fairly frequently says it helps him concentrate on creative matters. He says he's not sure how much it actually helps his PTSD. He feels *that* is a matter of effectively addressing the issues causing the PTSD; in other words, marijuana or any other drug is no replacement for the hard work necessary in recognizing why something is troubling an individual. But, still, he feels marijuana is a responsible, positive factor in his life.

Another veteran who has used marijuana off and on for decades sees its usage as positive for balancing out life's frustrations and difficulties. He laughs and says his wife will testify to how nice it makes him. But, he adds, it can be abused. "Too much of the stuff and it will make you stupid," he said. "What's important is to 'understand thyself,' then come to an understanding what effects, good and bad, marijuana has for you."

Who Is Profiting?

All it takes is listening to the incredible litany of horrific warnings about the side effects of legal pharmaceuticals in current TV advertisements to understand what he means. Everything can be abused and different people react to different things in different ways. The difference between legal drugs and illegal drugs is simple: One is legal and designed by a corporation to make money, while the other has been deemed illegal and, thus, is distributed by a criminalized class that makes the profits. One requires a cooperative doctor, and the other may get you locked up.

It's about ingesting a chemical that interacts with the body's chemistry. In the case of psychotropic drugs, this interaction shifts the balance of certain aspects of consciousness. The body doesn't care if the stuff is legal or illegal or who's making money off its use. If it has a benefit, that's good.

The Proposed Study of Marijuana as a PTSD Treatment

Rick Doblin is the moving force behind the marijuana study. He has a doctorate in public policy from Harvard. For years, he has worked to legalize marijuana. Once he got his PhD, he set up the Multidisciplinary Association for Psychedelic Studies (MAPS) in Santa Cruz, California. The study proposed by Dr. Doblin and MAPS would involve 50 combat veterans whose PTSD has not responded to other treatments. It would be a blind study with placebos.

To get a feel for Dr. Doblin, listen to him explaining his MAPS program at a conference in Israel, then at another in Canada and a third that addresses his long-term efforts to legalize marijuana.

Hard core drug warriors may smile and say, hey, this guy is a hippie! Doblin would probably give his trademark smirk. At one juncture in a video, he calls himself an "affirmative action hippie" they let into Harvard. He may smile easily, but the man is quite serious.

Widespread Need but Many Hurdles

"With so many veterans from the wars in Iraq and Afghanistan, there is a widely accepted need for a new treatment of PTSD," Doblin told the *Times*. "These are people whom we put in harm's way, and we have a moral obligation to help them."

So far, the Food and Drug Administration has OKed the study. The current hurdle is the Department of Health and Human Services, which must give the OK in order for Doblin and his team to obtain the marijuana for the study. It's not a matter of hooking up with a local dealer and obtaining the stuff. The marijuana has to come from the official US Government crop at the University of Mississippi.

If, instead of studying the beneficial aspects of marijuana, Dr. Doblin wanted to study its harmful effects, it's clear he would have a much easier time of it with the Feds.

Post-Traumatic Stress Disorder and the Military

If you are in the military, you may have seen combat. You may have been on missions that exposed you to horrible and life-threatening experiences. You may have been shot at, seen a buddy shot, or seen death. These are types of events that can lead to PTSD [post-traumatic stress disorder].

Experts think PTSD occurs:

- In about 11–20% of Veterans of the Iraq and Afghanistan wars (Operations Iraqi and Enduring Freedom), or in 11–20 Veterans out of 100.

- In as many as 10% of Gulf War (Desert Storm) Veterans, or in 10 Veterans out of 100.

- In about 30% of Vietnam Veterans, or about 30 out of 100 Vietnam Veterans.

Other factors in a combat situation can add more stress to an already stressful situation. This may contribute to PTSD and other mental health problems. These factors include what you do in the war, the politics around the war, where it's fought, and the type of enemy you face.

Another cause of PTSD in the military can be military sexual trauma (MST). This is any sexual harassment or sexual assault that occurs while you are in the military. MST can happen to both men and women and can occur during peacetime, training, or war.

Source: "How Common Is PTSD?,"
National Center for PTSD,
Department of Veterans Affairs, 2011.
www.ptsd.va.gov.

Getting to the Nitty Gritty

In his introductory remarks at the conference in Israel, Dr. Doblin gets to a key idea as to why asking questions about the benefits of marijuana use can be so troublesome to some. It has to do with the fact combat veterans are people trained and acculturated to war and its de-humanizing violence. It also has to do with a cultural addiction to violence and a fear of the unifying aspects of life.

"I'm not a psychologist or a therapist dealing with individual patients," he told the Israeli attendees. "I'm a public policy person dealing with sick public policies."

In his Israel remarks, he cites the rise of religious fundamentalism. He is fair and mentions all of the big three: Islam, Judaism and Christianity. "I think this rise of fundamentalism is pretty much the core problem in the world right now," he says. He means the separation and division of people from other people. He sees marijuana as a counter to this us-versus-them sense of difference between peoples that is so much an engine for violence and warfare.

"For many of us, psychedelics—and marijuana especially— have helped us have experiences of connection, mystical experiences where you feel part of everything, and that there's a deeper sense of identity than our religion or our country or our gender or our race; and that once you have this deeper sense of identity, you're more likely to be tolerant, you're more likely to appreciate differences rather than be scared by differences. And that's where peacemaking can come from."

The Process of Living

My wife has said for years the reason marijuana is illegal is that it makes an individual less in awe of power and authority and more in awe of the process of living and the beauty and joy that goes along with that process. For me, it has a lot to do with [famed psychiatrist Sigmund] Freud's idea of the life instinct versus the death instinct.

"[T]he inclination to aggression is an original, self-subsisting instinctual disposition in man," Freud writes in *Civilization and*

Its Discontents. This aggression, he says, "constitutes the greatest impediment to civilization."

He goes on to say "civilization is a process of *Eros*, whose purpose is to combine single human individuals, and after that, families, then races, peoples and nations, into one great unity, the unity of mankind. . . . [T]he struggle between *Eros* and Death, between the instinct of life and the instinct of destruction . . . is what all life essentially consists of."

Jungian analyst Loren E. Pedersen in *Dark Hearts: The Unconscious Forces That Shape Men's Lives* puts a Jungian [having to do with the theories of psychiatrist Carl Jung, who founded analytical psychology] spin on the destructive death instinct and sees it as the masculine focus on power as "a result of [men's] failure to incorporate the feminine in themselves."

Addressing the Unconscious

The point is, if we're going to seriously address issues of post-traumatic stress resulting from combat experience, the old, currently passé, notions of deep, unconscious forces at work in our day-to-day activities and decisions may be worth revisiting. And if something like a toke of marijuana helps inject a little *Eros* into a life stuck in the hell of death—that is a good thing.

The days of pure behaviorist manipulation and the treatment of mental problems with harsh, numbing prescription drugs may be in need of revision. The smiling Dr. Doblin may be right: Marijuana may help a troubled combat vet regain some sense of belonging to a greater species of humanity than that represented by the flag and the Marine Corps Hymn. But, then, we're back to the subversive quality of marijuana. But maybe some people need a little subversiveness to help them climb out of the hell they find themselves caught in.

Give Veterans Therapy That Works

In his fine book *War Is a Force That Gives Us Meaning*, war correspondent Chris Hedges nicely resurrects Freud's notion of *Eros* and *Thanatos*, the Greek term sometimes used for the death in-stinct. For Hedges, the former is "the impulse within us that pro-pels us to become close to others" and the latter is "the impulse that works toward the annihilation of all living things, including ourselves."

Soldiers in war can be traumatically overwhelmed by vio-lence and death. "The lust for violence, the freedom to eradicate the world around them, even human lives, is seductive," Hedges reports. "War ascendant wipes out *Eros*. War celebrates only power."

In the end, Dr. Doblin's proposal is not funny. It should be taken seriously and his team allowed what it needs to see if mari-juana is beneficial in easing the destructive impact of war on our veterans' lives. It's also bad policy to be criminalizing so many of our veterans who choose to "self-medicate" themselves. A little sanity in this area can go a long way.

"Obtaining [marijuana] from the federal government for research requires surmounting an extra regulatory hurdle that is not required for any other drug."

There Are Various Obstacles to Granting Medical Marijuana to Veterans

Brian Vastag

Brian Vastag is a reporter for the Washington Post. *In the following viewpoint, he highlights the bureaucratic and legal hurdles to granting medical marijuana to veterans suffering from post-traumatic stress disorder (PTSD). Vastag reports that although there is growing support for the option and a groundbreaking study proposed to investigate the benefits of medical marijuana, US government agencies, such as the Department of Health and Human Services (HHS), have strict control over selling government-grown marijuana. These agencies, Vastag explains, have not been flexible on the issue and treat marijuana differently than any other drug.*

Brian Vastag, "Marijuana Study of Traumatized Veterans Stuck in Regulatory Limbo," *Washington Post*, October 1, 2011. Copyright © 2011 by the Washington Post. All rights reserved. Reproduced by permission.

As you read, consider the following questions:

1. According to Vastag, how many Americans smoked marijuana in 2010?
2. According to a 2004 study in the *New England Journal of Medicine*, what percent of returning Iraq combat veterans had PTSD?
3. According to a 2008 report from the Rand Corporation, how many veterans will return from the Middle East clinically traumatized?

Getting pot on the street is easy. Just ask the 17 million Americans who smoked the federally illegal drug in 2010. Obtaining weed from the government? That's a lot harder.

A Groundbreaking Study

In April [2011], the Food and Drug Administration approved a first-of-its kind study to test whether marijuana can ease the nightmares, insomnia, anxiety and flashbacks common in combat veterans with post-traumatic stress disorder [PTSD].

But now another branch of the federal government has stymied the study. The Health and Human Services Department [HHS] is refusing to sell government-grown marijuana to the nonprofit group proposing the research, the Multidisciplinary Association for Psychedelic Studies.

The agency did leave the door open to eventually providing 13 pounds of the weed, which is grown at the University of Mississippi. But the HHS committee that rejected the request provided such conflicting criticisms that the person directing the study, MAPS Director Rick Doblin, is unsure how to address their concerns.

"Their goal at higher levels, I think, is to block the study," said Doblin, who for 25 years has been jumping through regulatory hoops to launch human studies of marijuana, LSD and MDMA, known as ecstasy, which are all illegal.

The HHS official in charge of the review, Sarah A. Wattenberg, declined to answer questions when reached by phone. Tara Broido, a spokeswoman for the agency, wrote in an e-mail that "the production and distribution of marijuana for clinical research is carefully restricted under a number of federal laws and international commitments."

PTSD and Marijuana

The study proposes testing five doses of marijuana in 50 combat veterans with PTSD whose symptoms have not improved despite conventional treatments—typically talk therapy, antidepressants and anti-anxiety medicines.

Many veterans already use marijuana to calm their PTSD, said Mary Tendall, a licensed therapist in Nevada City, Calif., who has treated "hundreds" of traumatized Vietnam, Afghanistan and Iraq veterans.

"It does mellow out the triggered response in a certain population," said Tendall, referring to hair-trigger anxiety reactions. "But with some, it made them very, very paranoid—it had the opposite effect."

Anecdotal Evidence

For Paul Culkin, a 32-year-old Army veteran living in Albuquerque, small daily doses of pot offer a release from sleepless nights and high anxiety.

In November 2004, Culkin suffered neck injuries when a car bomb exploded 30 feet from him in southern Kosovo.

When Culkin returned home, he had "really bad nightmares and insomnia, lots of cold sweats," he said. He rarely left the house.

Culkin began taking anti-depressants, and he eventually received a medical separation from the Army. He now receives Veterans Affairs disability payments.

New Mexico is one of two states, along with Delaware, that explicitly allows the use of marijuana to treat PTSD. Culkin got state approval in 2008 to use it. "It really gets rid of your night-mares if you smoke before you go to bed," he said. "You feel like you got some rest finally."

A Difficult Drug to Get

Doblin thinks marijuana can help many more veterans. A 2004 study in the *New England Journal of Medicine* estimated that 18 percent of returning Iraq combat veterans had PTSD. And a 2008 report from the Rand Corp., a government contractor, estimated that up to 225,000 veterans will return from the Middle East clinically traumatized.

Medical marijuana is legal in 16 states and the District of Columbia. But obtaining it from the federal government for research requires surmounting an extra regulatory hurdle that is not required for any other drug.

That's because one government agency, the National Institute on Drug Abuse, controls the nation's supply of research marijuana. Any non-government researcher wanting access to it needs to satisfy the special HHS committee.

On Sept. 14, Wattenberg, the official in charge of the committee, wrote to Doblin detailing "a number of concerns related to the proposal's approach, feasibility, and documentation of human subjects' protection."

A Myriad of Concerns

But written comments from the five committee members paint a jumbled picture of sometimes contradictory concerns.

One member wrote that the study should exclude veterans who have previously smoked marijuana. And another committee member asked for the opposite, that the study should only include people who have smoked the drug, as those naive to it might suffer anxiety or panic attacks.

A third reviewer wrote that study participants should be monitored closely—presumably in a hospital—rather than letting them smoke the marijuana at home.

"Turning this into an in-patient study ends the study," Doblin said. "Nobody will live in-patient for three months, and that increases the study costs astronomically."

Other comments expressed skepticism that the marijuana in the study—given in weekly batches—could be kept from getting "diverted," meaning given or sold to non-participants.

Too Much Bureaucracy

In a phone interview, Doblin pointed out that the study's design satisfied FDA drug-diversion officials.

Participants will be required to videotape their every interaction with the weed, and will have to return any they do not smoke. In addition, a second person will have to witness the smoking and check in with the researchers weekly.

Doblin plans to modify the study and resubmit it to the committee, which will have to unanimously agree before the marijuana sale can move forward, Broido said. But even if HHS approves, another bureaucracy looms—that of the Drug Enforcement Administration. The nation's drug cops also have to approve the research.

"It's a long road," Doblin said. "But it's worth it. We're the mythical American trying to play by the rules."

Periodical and Internet Sources Bibliography

The following articles have been selected to supplement the diverse views presented in this chapter.

Doug Bandow	"President Obama: Free the Medical Marijuana Researchers!," *Huffington Post*, December 13, 2009. www.huffingtonpost.com.
Amanda Burgess-Proctor	"Medical Marijuana Laws Expose Inconsistencies of US Drug Policy," *Morning Sun* (Central MI), October 5, 2011.
Andrew Cline	"Obama's Crazy Quilt Federalism," *American Spectator*, July 13, 2010.
Sue Major Holmes	"Medical Marijuana and PTSD: VA Doctors Can't Prescribe Pot Despite New Mexico's Promising Example," *Huffington Post*, March 13, 2010. www.huffingtonpost.com.
Paula Holmes-Greeley	"Easing the Pressure for Pot," *Muskegon Chronicle* (MI), May 26, 2010.
Asa Hutchinson	"Legalizing Marijuana Not Worth the Costs," CNBC, April 20, 2010. www.cnbc.com.
J. Patrick Pepper	"Medical Marijuana Behind the Smoke: Ogden Memo Says Feds Won't Go After Those Operating Within State Laws," *News-Herald* (MI), October 4, 2011.
Rob Reuteman	"The Confused State of Pot Law Enforcement," CNBC, April 20, 2010. www.cnbc.com.
USA Today	"Feds Won't Give Assurance on Medical Pot," July 1, 2011.
Chris Weigant	"Marijuana Prohibition's Legal Insanity Continues," *Huffington Post*, October 11, 2011. www.huffingtonpost.com.

CHAPTER 4

What Are Legal Issues for Patients Who Use Medical Marijuana?

Chapter Preface

In November 2009, Joe Casias, an employee at a Wal-Mart store in Battle Creek, Michigan, injured his knee while at work. Pursuant to Wal-Mart corporate policy, Casias was required to take a routine drug test to check for intoxicants and other substances. When the drug test came back, it showed that Casias tested positive for marijuana. In accordance with Wal-Mart's drug policy, Casias was promptly fired from his job, which he had held for five years.

However, Casias had traces of marijuana in his system because he was taking medical marijuana to treat the crippling pain he experienced every day from sinus cancer and an inoperable brain tumor pressing against his skull. It was his doctor who prescribed the drug, which is legal in Michigan for medicinal purposes, to alleviate the pain from the disease when traditional painkillers stopped working. Marijuana succeeded in easing some of his pain, and Casias was able to go to work, support his young family, and earn money to pay off his rising health care bills. According to Casias, he never came to work high, but instead used the marijuana to treat his pain after work when he was at home.

By all accounts, Casias was a model employee. He was named 2008 Associate of the Year at Wal-Mart. He also received positive performance awards. So when Casias informed Wal-Mart of the reason there was marijuana detected in his system that day—and showed them his legal medical marijuana card issued to him by the state of Michigan—he was surprised that he was fired. Many other medical marijuana supporters were also up in arms about Wal-Mart's decision. In light of the fact that medical marijuana is legal in the state, many people expected that Wal-Mart would be more lenient and take the unique circumstances of Casias's situation into account.

Wal-Mart stuck to its decision, however. As Wal-Mart corporate spokesperson Greg Rossiter explained to the media, "In states, such as Michigan, where prescriptions for marijuana can be obtained, an employer can still enforce a policy that requires termination of employment following a positive drug screen. We believe our policy complies with the law, and we support decisions based on the policy." Rossiter also cited safety concerns for customers and workers as justifications for Wal-Mart's actions.

Labor experts see more cases like Casias's popping up in states where medical marijuana is legal. Because the federal government has not legalized it, and has in fact claimed that there is no medicinal value in marijuana, there remains a legal gray area between federal and state medical marijuana drug policies. National corporations like Wal-Mart must take into account different drug laws in different states and also deal with liability issues involved in the matter. Many corporations have decided it is too risky to accommodate medical marijuana users and have opted to terminate their employment if medical marijuana use becomes known.

In Casias's case, he filed an appeal with the US District Court. On February 11, 2011, a federal judge upheld Wal-Mart's right to terminate his employment. In his opinion on the decision, Judge Robert Jonker argued that Michigan's medical marijuana law does not regulate private employment; it only protects Casias from criminal prosecution for using medical marijuana.

The controversy at the heart of the Casias case—how employers should treat employees using medical marijuana—is explored in the following chapter, which examines legal issues surrounding medical marijuana users such as job termination, arrest for drugged driving, and the right to own guns.

| "*Marijuana is a significant . . . contributing factor in a growing number of fatal accidents.*"

Medical Marijuana Users Are a Public Safety Risk on the Road

Ralph Vartabedian

Ralph Vartabedian is a reporter for the Los Angeles Times. *In the following viewpoint, he maintains that there is an unrecognized and growing crisis of drugged driving in the United States. This situation is exacerbated by the legalization of medical marijuana. Federal officials are conducting scientific research into the impairing effects of the drug. Vartabedian also reports that there is also a debate on establishing a national standard on the amount of the drug that drivers should be allowed to have in their blood. That debate is clouded by contradictory opinions on whether residual levels of marijuana can impair a driver days after the drug is smoked.*

As you read, consider the following questions:

1. According to the National Highway Traffic Safety Administration, what percentage of all drivers nationwide at night were high on marijuana?

2. How does the author say that police check to see if a driver is impaired?

3. What is marijuana's main ingredient, according to Vartabedian?

It was his green tongue that helped give away Jimmy Candido Flores when police arrived at the fatal accident scene near Chico.

Flores had run off the road and killed a jogger, Carrie Jean Holliman, a 56-year-old Chico elementary school teacher. California Highway Patrol officers thought he might be impaired and conducted a sobriety examination. Flores' tongue had a green coat typical of heavy marijuana users and a later test showed he had pot, as well as other drugs, in his blood.

After pleading guilty to manslaughter, Flores, a medical marijuana user, was sentenced in February to 10 years and 8 months in prison.

Holliman's death and others like it across the nation hint at what experts say is an unrecognized crisis: stoned drivers.

The Problem of Drugged Drivers

The most recent assessment by the National Highway Traffic Safety Administration, based on random roadside checks, found that 16.3% of all drivers nationwide at night were on various legal and illegal impairing drugs, half them high on marijuana.

In California alone, nearly 1,000 deaths and injuries each year are blamed directly on drugged drivers, according to CHP data, and law enforcement puts much of the blame on the rapid growth of medical marijuana use in the last decade. Fatalities in crashes where drugs were the primary cause and alcohol was not involved jumped 55% over the 10 years ending in 2009.

"Marijuana is a significant and important contributing factor in a growing number of fatal accidents," said Gil Kerlikowske, director of National Drug Control Policy in the White House and former Seattle police chief. "There is no question, not only from the data but from what I have heard in my career as a law enforcement officer."

As the medical marijuana movement has gained speed—one-third of the states now allow such sales—federal officials are pursuing scientific research into the impairing effects of the drug.

Zero Tolerance for Drugged Driving

The issue is compounded by the lack of a national standard on the amount of the drug that drivers should be allowed to have in their blood. While 13 states have adopted zero-tolerance laws, 35 states including California have no formal standard, and instead rely on the judgment of police to determine impairment.

Even the most cautious approach of zero tolerance is fraught with complex medical issues about whether residual low levels of marijuana can impair a driver days after the drug is smoked. Marijuana advocates say some state and federal officials are trying to make it impossible for individuals to use marijuana and drive legally for days or weeks afterward.

Marijuana is not nearly as well understood as alcohol, which has been the subject of statistical and medical research for decades.

"A lot of effort has gone into the study of drugged driving and marijuana, because that is the most prevalent drug, but we are not nearly to the point where we are with alcohol," said Jeffrey P. Michael, the National Highway Traffic Safety Administration's impaired-driving director. "We don't know what level of marijuana impairs a driver."

A Decisive Study

A $6-million study in Virginia Beach, Va., is attempting to remove any doubt that users of pot and other drugs are more likely to crash. Teams of federal researchers go to accident scenes and ask drivers to voluntarily provide samples of their blood. They later return to the same location, at the same time and on the same day of the week, asking two random motorists not involved in crashes for a blood sample.

The project aims to collect 7,500 blood samples to show whether drivers with specific blood levels of drugs are more likely to crash than those without the drugs, said John Lacey, a researcher at the nonprofit Pacific Institute for Research and Evaluation.

More Research Projects

In other projects, test subjects are being given marijuana to smoke and then examined under high-powered scanners or put in advanced driving simulators to gauge how it affects their brains and their ability to drive.

Federal scientists envision a day when police could quickly swab saliva from drivers' mouths and determine whether they have an illegal level of marijuana, but that will require years of research. Until then, police are in the same position they were with drunk driving in the 1950s, basing arrests on their professional judgment of each driver's behavior and vital signs.

If police suspect a driver is stoned, they now administer a lengthy 12-point examination. The driver must walk a straight line and stand on one leg, estimate the passage of 30 seconds and have pupils, blood pressure and pulse checked.

Chuck Hayes, national coordinator for the International Assn. of Chiefs of Police based in Washington, D.C., says the system works well to identify impaired drivers, and any future legal limit or medical test would be just another tool rather than a revolutionary change. "We are not concerned about levels or limits. We are concerned with impairment," Hayes said.

Establishing Standards

Indeed, even among law enforcement experts, the need for a standard is debated. Many support tried-and-true policing methods that can ferret out stoned drivers.

"Everybody wants a magic number, because that makes it easy," said Sarah Kerrigan, a toxicologist at Sam Houston State

University in Texas and an expert witness in numerous trials. "To have a law that says above a certain level you are impaired is not scientifically supportable. I don't think police need the tool, but my opinion may be in the minority."

But federal officials and local prosecutors argue that the lack of a standard makes convictions harder to obtain.

The Barraclough Case

In October [2010], a San Diego jury acquitted Terry Barraclough, a 60-year-old technical writer and medical marijuana user, on manslaughter charges in a fatal crash that occurred shortly after he had smoked marijuana.

A blood test showed he had high levels of active marijuana ingredients in his blood, but the jury heard conflicting expert testimony from toxicologists about the possible effects.

Martin Doyle, the deputy district attorney who prosecuted Barraclough, said the acquittal showed that the lack of a formal legal limit on marijuana intoxication makes such prosecutions tough.

"We don't have a limit in California and that made my prosecution very difficult," Doyle said. "We have a lapse in the law."

But defense attorney Michael Cindrich said the failed prosecution shows that the San Diego district attorney was targeting medical marijuana users and that any legal limit would be unfair to the people who rely on the drug to treat their problems.

Indeed, Anthony Cardoza, an attorney who represented Flores in the Chico accident, said his client was not impaired and that allegations about his green tongue were ridiculous. Flores' guilty plea was prompted by other legal issues, including a prior conviction for a drunk driving accident that caused an injury.

The Effects of Marijuana

Marilyn Huestis, a toxicologist and one of the nation's top experts on marijuana at the National Institute on Drug Abuse who is directing several research programs, said she believed there is

Why Is Drugged Driving Hazardous?

THC [the active compound in Marijuana] affects areas of the brain that control the body's movements, balance, coordination, memory, and judgment, as well as sensations. Because these effects are multifaceted, more research is required to understand marijuana's impact on the ability of drivers to react to complex and unpredictable situations. However, we do know that—

- A meta-analysis of approximately 60 experimental studies—including laboratory, driving simulator, and on-road experiments—found that behavioral and cognitive skills related to driving performance were impaired in a dose-dependent fashion with increasing THC blood levels.

- Evidence from both real and simulated driving studies indicates that marijuana can negatively affect a driver's attentiveness, perception of time and speed, and ability to draw on information obtained from past experiences.

- A study of over 3,000 fatally injured drivers in Australia showed that when marijuana was present in the blood of the driver, he or she was much more likely to be at fault for the accident. Additionally, the higher the THC concentration, the more likely the driver was to be culpable.

- Research shows that impairment increases significantly when marijuana use is combined with alcohol. Studies have found that many drivers who test positive for alcohol also test positive for THC, making it clear that drinking and drugged driving are often linked behaviors.

Source: "Drugged Driving," National Institute on Drug Abuse, 2011.

no amount of marijuana that a person can consume and drive safely immediately afterward.

Supporters of marijuana legalization agree that the drug can impair a driver, but argue that the effects wear off in a few hours. Huestis, however, said research was showing that the effects of marijuana can linger.

Marijuana's main ingredient—delta-9 THC—stays in the blood for an hour or more and then breaks down into metabolites that are both psychoactive and inert. But the impairing effects can linger, even after the THC is no longer in the blood, Huestis said. Because it can be absorbed into body tissue and slowly released for days, Huestis believes that heavy chronic daily users may be impaired in ways that are not yet understood.

A complicating factor is the tendency of many marijuana users to also use alcohol, which can sharply amplify impairment. Very little research has been conducted to determine whether it is possible to set limits on a combination of such substances.

Punishing Marijuana Users

Paul Armentano, deputy director for the National Organization for the Reform of Marijuana Laws, said some states had laws that can punish users even when they are not high, pointing to a tough Arizona statute that allows conviction for impaired driving when an inert metabolite is detected in the blood.

Arizona officials said they wrote the law because there was no scientific agreement on how long marijuana impairs a driver. But proponents see something more sinister: an effort to put marijuana users in constant legal jeopardy.

"We are not setting a standard based on impairment, but one similar to saying that if you have one sip of alcohol you are too drunk to drive for the next week," Armentano said.

"While it is well established that alcohol consumption increases accident risk, evidence of marijuana's culpability in on-road driving accidents and injury is far less clear."

Marijuana Users and Law Enforcement Must Be Educated to Ensure Safe Driving

Paul Armentano

Paul Armentano is the deputy director of the National Organization for the Reform of Marijuana Laws (NORML). In the following viewpoint, he maintains that while there are questions regarding the degree to which marijuana impairs driving performance, experts believe that it has less of an effect than alcohol and many prescription drugs. However, the author asserts, drivers should never operate motor vehicles in an impaired condition. Armentano suggests that public awareness campaigns geared toward the younger driving population focus on the risks of drugged driving, especially the risk of using cannabis in combinations with alcohol or other illicit drugs. Law enforcement officers should also be better trained

Paul Armentano, "Cannabis and Driving: A Scientific and Rational Review," NORML.org, January 7, 2011. Copyright © 2011 by the National Organization for the Reform of Marijuana Laws. All rights reserved. Reproduced by permission.

to identify drivers under the influence of marijuana, Armentano contends.

As you read, consider the following questions:

1. According to Armentano, how many Americans said that they operated a motor vehicle while under the influence of an illicit substance in 2006?
2. What does the author cite as the most prevalent illicit drug detected in fatally injured drivers and motor vehicle crash victims?
3. According to a 2004 study published in *Accident, Analysis and Prevention*, what two substances caused drivers to experience an increased crash risk?

Policy debates regarding marijuana law reform invariably raise the question: "How does society address concerns regarding pot use and driving?" The subject is worthy of serious discussion. NORML's Board of Directors addressed this issue by ratifying a "no driving" clause to the organization's "Principles of Responsible Cannabis Use" stating, "Although cannabis is said by most experts to be safer with motorists than alcohol and many prescription drugs, responsible cannabis consumers never operate motor vehicles in an impaired condition."

Nevertheless, questions remain regarding the degree to which smoking cannabis impairs actual driving performance. Unlike alcohol, which is known to increase drivers' risk-taking behavior and is a primary contributor in on-road accidents, marijuana's impact on psychomotor skills is subtle and its real-world impact in automobile crashes is conflicting.

Drugged Driving: True Threat or False Panic?

Survey data indicates that approximately 112 million Americans (46 percent of the US population) have experimented with the use of illicit substances. Of these, more than 20 million (8.3 percent of the population) self-identify as "current" or "monthly" users of illicit drugs, and more than 10 million Americans say that they've operated a motor vehicle while under the influence of an illicit substance in the past year [2006]. These totals, while far from negligible, suggest that the prevalence of illicit drug use among US drivers is far less than the prevalence of alcohol among this same population.

To date, "[The] role of drugs as a causal factor in traffic crashes involving drug-positive drivers is still not well understood." While some studies have indicated that illicit drug use is associated with an increased risk of accident, a relationship has not been established regarding the use of psychoactive substances and crash severity. Drivers under the influence of illicit drugs do experience an enhanced fatality risk compared to sober drivers. However, this risk is approximately three times lower than the fatality risk associated with drivers who operate a vehicle above or near the legal limit for alcohol intoxication. According to one recent review: "The risk of all drug-positive drivers compared to drug-free drivers is similar to drivers with a blood alcohol concentration of 0.05%. The risk is also similar to drivers above age 60 compared to younger drivers [around age 35]."

Marijuana is the most common illicit substance consumed by motorists who report driving after drug use. Epidemiological research also indicates that cannabis is the most prevalent illicit drug detected in fatally injured drivers and motor vehicle crash victims. Reasons for this are twofold. One, pot is by far the most widely used illicit drug among the US population, with nearly one out of two Americans admitting having tried it. Two, marijuana is the most readily detectable illicit drug in toxicological tests. Marijuana's primary psychoactive compound, THC, may be detected in blood for several hours, and in some extreme cases days after past use, long after any impairing effects have worn off. In addition, non-psychoactive byproducts of cannabis, known as metabolites, may be detected in the urine of regular users for days or weeks after past use. (Other common drugs of abuse, such as cocaine or methamphetamine, do not possess such long half-lives.) Therefore, pot's prevalence in toxicological evaluations of US drivers does not necessarily indicate that it is a frequent or significant causal factor in auto accidents. Rather, its prevalence affirms that cannabis remains far more popular and is far more easily detectable on drug screening tests than other controlled substances.

Cruising on Cannabis: Clarifying the Debate

While it is well established that alcohol consumption increases accident risk, evidence of marijuana's culpability in on-road driving accidents and injury is far less clear. Although acute cannabis intoxication following smoking has been shown to mildly impair psychomotor skills, this impairment is seldom severe or long lasting. In closed course and driving simulator studies, marijuana's acute effects on psychomotor performance include minor impairments in tracking (eye movement control) and reaction time, as well as variation in lateral positioning, headway (drivers under the influence of cannabis tend to follow less closely to the vehicle in front of them), and speed (drivers tend to decrease speed following cannabis inhalation). In general, these variations in driving behavior are noticeably less consistent or pronounced than the impairments exhibited by subjects under the influence of alcohol. Also, unlike subjects impaired by alcohol, individuals under the influence of cannabis tend to be aware of their impairment and try to compensate for it accordingly, either by driving more cautiously or by expressing an unwillingness to drive altogether.

As a result, cannabis-induced variations in performance do not appear to play a significant role in on-road traffic accidents when THC levels in a driver's blood are low and/or cannabis is not consumed in combination with alcohol. For example, a 1992 National Highway Traffic Safety Administration review of the

Teen Driving Facts

Motor vehicle crashes are the leading cause of death for 15- to 20-year-olds. Drugs, alcohol, and driver distractions increase teens' crash risks. As teens take to the roads, parents can take action by talking about the dangers of drunk, drugged, and distracted driving.

Teens are at risk—both from driving under the influence of drugs or alcohol and from riding with drivers who are under the influence.

- Thirteen percent of high school seniors reported driving under the influence of marijuana in the prior two weeks, a number nearly equivalent to those who reported driving under the influence of alcohol (14%), despite higher prevalence of alcohol consumption among teens.

- High school students are more likely to drink, smoke cigarettes, and smoke marijuana after earning their driver's license.

- In a comprehensive study on unsafe driving by high school students, 30 percent of seniors reported driving after drinking heavily or using drugs, or riding in a car whose driver had been drinking heavily or using drugs, at least once in the prior two weeks.

- Next to marijuana, prescription drugs are the most commonly abused illicit drug by teens. The most commonly abused prescription drugs act on systems in the brain that can lead to impaired driving ability, making them harmful to young drivers when abused and mixed with alcohol or other illicit drugs.

Source: "Teen Driving Facts," National Youth Anti-Drug Media Campaign, 2011.

role of drug use in fatal accidents reported, "There was no indication that cannabis itself was a cause of fatal crashes" among drivers who tested positive for the presence of the drug. A more recent assessment by Blows and colleagues noted that self-reported recent use of cannabis (within three hours of driving) was not significantly associated with car crash injury after investigators controlled for specific cofounders (e.g., seat-belt use, sleepiness, etc.). A 2004 observational case control study published in the journal *Accident, Analysis and Prevention* reported that only drivers under the influence of alcohol or benzodiazepines experience an increased crash risk compared to drug-free controls. Investigators did observe increased risks—though they were not statistically significant—among drivers using amphetamines, cocaine and opiates, but found, "No increased risk for road trauma was found for drivers exposed to cannabis."

An Elevated Risk

A handful of more recent studies have noted a positive association between very recent cannabis exposure and a gradually increased risk of vehicle accident. Typically, these studies reveal that drivers who possess THC/blood concentrations above 5ng/ml —implying cannabis inhalation within the past 1–3 hours— experience an elevated risk of accident compared to drug-free controls. (Motorists who test positive for the presence of THC in the blood at concentrations below this threshold typically do not have an increased risk compared to controls.) However, this elevated risk is below the risk presented by drivers who have consumed even small quantities of alcohol.

Two recent case-controlled studies have assessed this risk in detail. A 2007 case-control study published in the *Canadian Journal of Public Health* reviewed 10 years of US auto-fatality data. Investigators found that US drivers with blood alcohol levels of 0.05%—a level well below the legal limit for intoxication— were three times as likely to have engaged in unsafe driving activities prior to a fatal crash as compared to individuals who tested positive for marijuana. A 2005 review of auto accident fatality data from France showed similar results, finding that drivers who tested positive for any amount of alcohol had a four times greater risk of having a fatal accident than did drivers who tested positive for marijuana in their blood. In the latter study, even drivers with low levels of alcohol present in their blood (below 0.05%) experienced a greater elevated risk as compared to drivers who tested positive for high concentrations of cannabis (above 5ng/ml). Both studies noted that overall few traffic accidents appeared to be attributed to drivers operating a vehicle while impaired by cannabis.

Defining a Rational "Drugged Driving" Policy

The above review illustrates the need for further education and understanding regarding the effects of cannabis upon driving behavior. While pot's adverse impact on psychomotor skills is less severe than the effects of alcohol, driving under the acute influence of cannabis still may pose an elevated risk of accident in certain situations. However, because marijuana's psychomotor impairment is subtle and short-lived, consumers can greatly reduce this risk by refraining from driving for a period of several hours following their cannabis use.

By contrast, motorists should never be encouraged to operate a vehicle while smoking cannabis. Drivers should also be advised that engaging in the simultaneous use of both cannabis and alcohol can significantly increase their risk of accident compared to the consumption of either substance alone. Past use of cannabis, as defined by the detection of inactive cannabis metabolites in the urine of drivers, is not associated with an increased accident risk.

Educating Young Drivers

Educational or public service campaigns targeting drugged driving behavior should particularly be aimed toward the younger driving population age 16 to 25—as this group is most likely to use cannabis and report having operated a motor vehicle shortly after consuming pot. In addition, this population may have less driving experience, may be more prone to engage in risk-taking behavior, and may be more naïve to pot's psychoactive effects than older, more experienced populations. This population also reports a greater likelihood for having driven after using cannabis in combinations with other illicit drugs or alcohol. Such an educational campaign was recently launched nationwide in Canada by the Canadian Public Health Association and could readily be replicated in the United States. Arguably, such a campaign would enjoy enhanced credibility if coordinated by a private public health association or traffic safety organization, such as the American Public Health Association or the AAA Automobile Club, as opposed to the federal Office of National Drug Control Policy—whose previous public service campaigns have demonstrated limited influence among younger audiences.

Finally, increased efforts should be made within the law enforcement community to train officers and DREs (drug recognition experts) to better identify drivers who may be operating a vehicle while impaired by marijuana. In Australia, efforts have been made to adapt elements of the roadside Standardized Field Sobriety Test to make it sensitive to drivers who may be under the influence of cannabis. Scientific evaluations of these tests have shown that subjects' performance on the modified SFSTs may be positively associated with dose-related levels of marijuana impairment. Similarly, clinical testing for cannabis impairment among suspected drugged drivers in Norway has been positively associated with identifying drivers with THC/blood concentrations above 3ng/ml.

Though the development of such cannabis-specific impairment testing is still in its infancy, an argument may be made for the provisional use of such tests by specially trained members of law enforcement. In addition, the development of cannabis-sensitive technology to rapidly identify the presence of THC in drivers, such as a roadside saliva test, would provide utility to law enforcement in their efforts to better identify intoxicated drivers. The development of such technology would also increase public support for the taxation and regulation of cannabis by helping to assuage concerns that liberalizing marijuana policies could potentially lead to an increase in incidences of drugged driving. Such concerns are a significant impediment to the enactment of marijuana law reform, and must be sufficiently addressed before a majority of the public will embrace any public policy that proposes regulating adult cannabis use like alcohol.

"The ATF is absolutely correct in its interpretation. Admitted stoners cannot buy guns. Period."

Medical Marijuana Users Should Be Barred from Purchasing Firearms

Peter Bella

Peter Bella is a freelance writer and photographer. In the following viewpoint, he discusses how to treat medical marijuana users seeking to buy firearms in states with medical marijuana laws. Bella blames the states for the problem, contending that they did not seek waivers from the federal government on the issue of firearms nor did they seek a clarification from the Bureau of Alcohol, Tobacco, Firearms and Explosives (ATF) before legislation was passed. Therefore, Bella concludes, the states will have to find a workable solution to what has become a major problem.

As you read, consider the following questions:

1. According to Bella, how many states have legalized medical marijuana as of October 2011?
2. How does the author describe the ATF?

3. How did the Oregon Supreme Court rule on the issue of selling gun permits to admitted marijuana users, according to Bella?

Medical marijuana is legal in Montana and several other states. People who want to get stoned can obtain state issued medical ID cards to legally buy an illegal substance. Then Montana firearm dealers opened up Pandora's box of political insanity when they contacted the ATF [US Bureau of Alcohol, Tobacco, Firearms and Explosives] about people who possessed medical marijuana cards or who admitted marijuana use on their firearm purchase forms and that wanted to buy guns.

Under federal law it is illegal to sell a firearm to anyone who admits to using, or is addicted to, federally illegal controlled substances.

Sixteen states, plus the District of Columbia, have legalized a substance that is banned by the federal government, setting off the law of unintended consequences.

Under federal law, cannabis is a Schedule 1 controlled substance. It cannot be cultivated, possessed, prescribed, dispensed, distributed, or sold. The United States Supreme Court ruled that the federal government has the right to regulate and criminalize Cannabis. (*United States v. Oakland Cannabis Buyers' Coop* and *Gonzales v. Raich*)

Since sixteen states have legalized so-called medical marijuana, there have been increases in two things: the numbers of people who purportedly claim illnesses supposedly eased by marijuana use, and the numbers of producers and sellers of the cash crop.

Those Montana firearms dealers were merely trying to protect themselves and their businesses. They sought clarification. ATF's response was fast and furious. No way. No how. It was the correct interpretation.

Besides being a law enforcement agency, ATF is a regulatory agency. They regulate the trade in alcohol, tobacco, and fire-

Excerpt of ATF Memo on Gun Rights

Federal law, 18 U.S.C. § 922(g)(3), prohibits any person who is an "unlawful user of or addicted to any controlled substance (as defined in section 102 of the Controlled Substances Act (21 U.S.C. 802))" from shipping, transporting, receiving or possessing firearms or ammunition. Marijuana is listed in the Controlled Substances Act as a Schedule I controlled substance, and there are no exceptions in Federal law for marijuana purportedly used for medicinal purposes, even if such use is sanctioned by State law. Further, Federal law, 18 U.S.C. § 922(d)(3), makes it unlawful for any person to sell or otherwise dispose of any firearm or ammunition to any person knowing or having reasonable cause to believe that such person is an unlawful user of or addicted to a controlled substance. As provided by 27 C.F.R. § 478.11, "an inference of current use may be drawn from evidence of a recent use or possession of a controlled substance or a pattern of use or possession that reasonably covers the present time."

Therefore, any person who uses or is addicted to marijuana, regardless of whether his or her State has passed legislation authorizing marijuana use for medicinal purposes, is an unlawful user of or addicted to a controlled substance, and is prohibited by Federal law from possessing firearms or ammunition.

Arthur Herbert, "Open Letter to All Federal Firearms Licensees," Bureau of Alcohol, Tobacco, Firearms and Explosives, September 21, 2011.

arms, hence their name, "Alcohol, Tobacco, and Firearms (and Explosives)." Licensed gun dealers must keep meticulous records that make CPAs [certified public accountants] look slipshod. Those records are subject to inspection at any time by the ATF.

Owning and operating a firearm dealership requires a major financial investment. ATF can put you out of business in a heartbeat. You can also be fined or prosecuted for violations of the laws regulating the sales of firearms. Firearm dealers fear the ATF more than the IRS [Internal Revenue Service].

In order to purchase a firearm, consumers must check off several boxes on a purchase form. One of the boxes asks if you use or are addicted to controlled substances. If you check yes, you are denied the purchase. If you lie and check no, you walk out of the store with your shiny new toy. We can see a problem right there.

But it gets tricky. The federal government does not acknowledge the legalization of medical marijuana by states. It even gets trickier. The [President Barack] Obama administration, until two months ago, decided to ignore the whole issue.

This left gun dealers in a quandary. Besides being licensed by the federal government, they have state and local business licenses. As anyone in business knows, the last thing you want to do is get the local politicians and bureaucrats mad at you. Refusing to sell guns to people who are authorized by the state to use a federal illegal substance would cause all kinds of local trouble.

Being responsible businesspeople, they sought guidance from the government agency that regulates them, the ATF. The response is that they not only can, but must refuse to sell firearms to anyone who claims to use marijuana for any reason.

The fault of this problem lies with the states who legalized marijuana. OK, call it medical marijuana if it makes the stoners happy. They knew and were warned that marijuana is an illegal controlled substance.

They ignored the law and the warnings.

Oregon is facing a similar problem. Sheriffs are refusing to issue gun permits to people who admitted using medical marijuana citing federal law. The Oregon Supreme Court ruled that the state had to issue the permits, though they cannot force dealers to sell guns. The case is now on appeal through the federal court system.

The federal gun laws are what they are. The federal drug laws are what they are. The ATF is absolutely correct in its interpretation. Admitted stoners cannot buy guns. Period.

Montana and the other states did not heed the warnings of the federal government when they knowingly passed laws that were in direct conflict with federal drug laws. They did not consult with or seek waivers from the federal government when they knew full well people who use illegal controlled substances cannot purchase firearms.

This is a problem they created for themselves and they have to live with it. They openly flouted federal law by legalizing an illegal substance. Had they performed due diligence this problem could have been alleviated before they passed their laws. The state politicians are responsible for the mess they created.

[Montana attorney general Steve] Bullock, and officials in other states where this is a problem, doth protest too much. They created the mess. They need to fix it.

"*It is egregious that people may be
sentenced to years in a federal prison
only because they possessed a firearm
while using state-approved medicine.*"

Medical Marijuana Users Should Not Have to Give Up Their Gun Rights

Phillip Smith

Phillip Smith is a writer for the Drug War Chronicle. *In the following viewpoint, he reports on the efforts of medical marijuana supporters to defend the gun rights of patients against the Bureau of Alcohol, Tobacco, Firearms and Explosives (ATF), a government agency that recently directed firearms dealers to deny guns to anyone with a medical marijuana registration card. Smith finds that many pro-marijuana activists are vigorously demanding the reinstatement of gun rights for medical marijuana users as well as a comprehensive medical marijuana policy from the President Barack Obama administration that respects the rights of patients and treats medical marijuana as a public health issue. According to Smith, many activists believe that fighting the issue in the courts is the only way to strike a decisive victory in the battle.*

As you read, consider the following questions:

1. How does Dale Gieringer characterize the Obama administration's approach to medical marijuana?
2. What was the response of the National Rifle Association to the ATF position, according to Smith?
3. According to the author, what was the ruling in the *Willis v. Winters* case in Oregon?

In a memo released last week [September 21, 2011], the US Department of Justice has notified federal firearms dealers that medical marijuana patients are "addicts" or "unlawful drug users" who cannot legally own weapons or ammunition. A medical marijuana registration card is proof enough to deny a weapons sale, the memo said. That has medical marijuana advocates crying foul, but national gun rights groups—not so much.

The Herbert Memo

The memo was authored by Arthur Herbert, Assistant Director for Enforcement Programs and Services for the Bureau of Alcohol, Tobacco, and Firearms (ATF). Herbert said he wrote the memo after receiving "a number of inquiries about the use of marijuana for medical purposes, and its applicability to federal firearms laws."

Herbert cited the section of the federal criminal code that prohibits anyone who is "an unlawful user of or addicted to any controlled substance" from possessing firearms. He reminded firearms dealers that they cannot legally sell guns to people they have reasonable cause to believe are illegal drug users or addicts and wrote that anyone presenting a medical marijuana registration card is providing reasonable cause for the dealer to believe they are illegal drug users or addicts.

Despite the [President Barack] Obama administration's 2009 Justice Department memo famously vowing not to go after patients and providers in compliance with state laws, the federal government has never wavered from its stance that despite state medical marijuana laws, marijuana remains a Schedule I controlled substance.

"Any person who uses or is addicted to marijuana, regardless of whether not his or her state has passed legislation authorizing marijuana use for medicinal purposes, is an unlawful user of or is addicted to a controlled substance and is prohibited by federal law from possessing firearms or ammunition," Herbert wrote.

A Concern for Gun Rights

While the federal gun law is not new, its restatement with specific reference to medical marijuana patients is, and that has advocates concerned.

"This is more evidence of the Obama administration's malfeasance with regard to medical marijuana," said Dale Gieringer, long-time director of California NORML [National Organization for the Reform of Marijuana Laws]. "They have a real penchant for over-regulation. We've seen it with the Treasury rules and warnings to banks, we've seen it with the continued arrests by other federal agencies. What's particularly disturbing is that this memo comes from a Justice Department that three years ago said it was going to respect state laws regarding medical marijuana."

"I don't think the feds are going to go after gun dealers selling to medical marijuana patients, but the important thing is that if you use this medicine your constitutional rights are forfeit," said Morgan Fox, communications director for the Marijuana Policy Project. "This is just a travesty. Trying to treat medical marijuana patients like second-class citizens and stripping them of their rights as they are dealing with illness is just despicable."

Demonizing the Patient Community

"The possession of a firearm could make a medical marijuana patient vulnerable to additional charges and sentencing if convicted of a federal marijuana crime, and patients should be aware of that," said Kris Hermes, spokesman for Americans for Safe Access. "However, it is not the federal government's place to prevent medical marijuana patients from owning firearms. Following in the footsteps of the Justice Department, Veterans Affairs, and Housing and Urban Development, the ATF memo illustrates how yet another arm of the Obama Administration has demonized medical marijuana and the patient community. The ATF memo underscores the need for a comprehensive policy from the Obama administration that treats medical marijuana as the public health issue that it is," Hermes concluded.

While medical marijuana supporters have expressed outrage, groups that can usually be counted on to stand up for Second Amendment rights have been largely silent. Although the National Shooting Sports Foundation was the first place outside ATF to post the open letter, it has not responded to repeated *Chronicle* requests to comment on the Second Amendment rights of medical marijuana users. Neither has the National Rifle Association.

A National Gun Rights Group Responds

After this article went to publication, Gun Owners of America executive director Larry Pratt belatedly replied to our requests for comment.

"ATF seems to be dazed now that their Fast & Furious accessory-to-murder scheme has come to light," Pratt said. "Their first blind punch was the demand letter regarding multiple rifle sales in the four southwest border states. Not only is it a stupid attempt to try to blame gun stores for what ATF was telling them to do (or doing it directly themselves), but it is illegal. Now they want FFLs [Federal Firearms Licenses] to profile gun buyers to guess who looks like a marijuana user. Again, they have no legal authority to ask for such an impossibility. What's not to like?"

Private Firearm Ownership in the US, 2010		
	Percentage	*Number*
Households With a Gun	40–45%	47–53 million
Adults Owning a Gun	30–34%	70–80 million
Adults Owning a Handgun	17–19%	40–45 million

TAKEN FROM: James D. Agresti and Reid K. Smith, "Fun Control Facts," *Just Facts*, September 13, 2010. Revised 11/18/11. http://justfacts.com/guncontrol.asp.

The Situation in Montana

One exception is Montana, where both medical marijuana and gun rights are perennial hot topics. There, patients and firearms enthusiasts seem to on the same page.

"It is egregious that people may be sentenced to years in a federal prison only because they possessed a firearm while using a state-approved medicine," said Gary Marbut, president of the Montana Shooting Sports Association.

"This is making people pretty crazy here in Montana," said Kate Chowela of the Montana Cannabis Industry Association. "This is a gun owning state, hunting is a big part of our tradition, we have that whole independent frontier thing going on. The government is rescinding the Second Amendment rights of people who use marijuana for their medical conditions. We have had the feeling that this was the policy, but now that we see it in writing for the first time, that really cements it," she added.

A Chance to Amend Policy

The policy may be cemented, but that doesn't mean the law on Second Amendment rights for medical marijuana patients is set in stone.

"It's all well and good for a federal agency to tell us what they think the law is, and that's what ATF has done," said Keith Stroup, founder and current counsel for NORML. "But there is no federal or state court decision that has held a medical marijuana patient is disqualified from owning a gun."

"This breaks down like Justice Department opinion in general. They say they have a legal right to deny gun ownership, but they can't force the states to comply with that; they'll just have to enforce the law themselves," Fox said. "This is just a restatement of policy; there have been no court battles over it yet."

Judicial Challenges

There could be one coming. In a case decided in May, *Willis v. Winters*, the Oregon Supreme Court upheld circuit and appeals court rulings that the Jackson and Washington county sheriffs could not deny concealed weapons permits to medical marijuana patients. The Oregon Sheriffs' Association has now petitioned the US Supreme Court, which will consider whether to take up the appeal in an October 7 conference.

"In the Oregon concealed handgun cases, we argued that medical marijuana patients are not 'illegal drug users or addict' as that term is used in federal law, based on the legislative history of the law," explained attorney Leland Berger, who argued the case. "The Oregon sheriffs have petitioned the US Supreme Court for certiori," Berger said. "I wrote the court saying that the cases were not certiori worthy and that we waived a response to the petition unless they asked us to file one."

In the meantime, CANORML's Gieringer had some common sense advice for patients and dispensary operators. "If you're a medical marijuana patient, don't mention it when you go buy a gun," recommended Gieringer. But he had a word of warning for dispensary operators. "I assume the feds will be ready to use this if they are prosecuting a dispensary and there were any guns on board," he said.

"If the prevailing medical marijuana movement can win its first high profile employee discrimination case . . . then it is well on its way to winning the war."

Employees Should Not Be Fired for Using Medical Marijuana

Kelley Vlahos

Kelley Vlahos is a writer and contributor to the American Conservative. *In the following viewpoint, she cites the case of Joseph Casias, a Michigan man fired by his employer, Wal-Mart, when he failed a company drug test that showed traces of medically prescribed marijuana. Vlahos defends Casias, pointing out that marijuana is legal for medicinal use in Michigan and that Casias was unfairly treated by Wal-Mart, which fired him and tried to prevent him from getting unemployment benefits. Vlahos detects a political angle, associating Wal-Mart with a group of Republicans that oppose the use of medical marijuana, and views Casias as a landmark case of medical marijuana and labor rights in today's workplace.*

As you read, consider the following questions:

1. How many million Americans does Wal-Mart employ, according to the author?
2. What percentage of Michigan voters does Vlahos say voted to pass the Medicinal Marijuana Act in 2008?
3. According to the author, how many Michigan residents have applied for medical marijuana cards?

The medical marijuana movement has hit *the* wall of resistance. It is in the form of one Joseph Casias, a 29-year-old father of two with a brain tumor and sinus cancer who was fired by Wal-Mart for testing positive for marijuana in his system. The State of Michigan says he is allowed to smoke marijuana to ease his chronic pain. Wal-Mart says too bad. It is now Casias' turn to bring it to court.

The Power of Wal-Mart

To think about it, it probably makes sense that any major progress in the movement—and towards ultimately ending the War on Drugs—would involve winning a titular battle against Wal-Mart, the socially conservative bastion of globalization's crudest but most cardinal rewards (cheap stuff, cheap labor and ever-expanding commercial hegemony), which has become synonymous with American culture, industry and even politics. It also employs 1.4 million Americans and runs some 4,300 stores (including Sam's Clubs) world-wide.

In other words, if the prevailing medical marijuana movement can win its first high profile employee discrimination case—one that involves Wal-Mart Inc.—then it is well on its way to winning the war.

If not, it could be a fatal blow. Because no matter how far the politics and the law has come regarding the ability for sick people to access medical marijuana in their state without prosecution, if the nation's largest private employer isn't on board, their medical cards won't be worth the paper they're written on.

Let's face it, the days of "Stop the Wal" are already in the rear-view. Politically well-connected and at least partly responsible for the 10-year $186 billion trade deficit with China, Wal-Mart has positioned itself artfully as the savior of modest households strapped by the current recession. In fact they've profited from it. Families can *buy more, for less* (emphasis on more), including food and cheap prescription drugs, at Wal-Mart—and 64 percent of Americans in the last three months have, according to statistics.

And with so many Americans on the payroll, Wal-Mart has its big old thumb on a lot of (struggling) communities nationwide. One big happy family.

David and Goliath

Except of course for Casias, who lives in Battle Creek, Michigan. Reflecting the unreconstructed tone of the Republican establishment it has long identified with, Wal-Mart has in effect taken a stand against Michigan's new medical marijuana law and has unceremoniously tossed Casias—one of its vaunted salt-of-the-earth American "associates"—into the street like so much rubbish.

Now Casias finds himself in a formidable, but probably an unenviable position, having to decide whether to test one of the country's most comprehensive medical marijuana laws against one of the only places still employing his friends and neighbors in Battle Creek.

But if Goliath can be brought to heel in this epic War on Drugs, to prove that yes, the will of the people in one state supercedes even the biggest global corporate behemoth, then maybe guys like Joe Casias won't have to choose between their job security and relieving their physical pain, between the well-being of their families and the personal choice not to medicate with narcotics and psychotropic drugs.

Joe Casias

For 11 years, Casias has been living with sinus cancer, which has gotten so bad that it makes his voice sound so painfully obstructed that it is difficult to understand what he is saying. He looks older than his 29 years, his face drawn, his body rail-thin. He is a father of two young children, ages 7 and 8. It is difficult not to get emotionally drawn into his painful story.

Casias has been working at Wal-Mart for five years and was such a model employee that at one point had been named "associate of the year." Last fall he was promoted—a proud moment for Casias—which allowed him to finally enroll in the company's self-funded health care plan. Up to that point, he had been one of the nation's 40-plus [million] uninsured and was swimming in medical bills and struggling to keep up with collection agency payment plans.

One day during November, he sprained his knee on the job and after being directed to the emergency room for care, was put through a company-mandated drug test. He tested positive for marijuana because for at least four months, Casias had been smoking marijuana—which *is legally sanctioned in the State of Michigan*—to relieve his chronic pain in lieu of prescription pain killers.

Claiming that Casias had violated the company's zero-tolerance drug policy, Wal-Mart fired him on the spot—five years and several pounds of flesh snuffed in an instant.

"I never went to work under the influence—I would never do that," Casias told me in an interview from home last week. "I gave them everything I got."

A Legal Drug

But smoking, he said, allowed him to avoid the pills, which he said were habit forming and had nasty side effects. Coincidentally, 63 percent of Michigan voters felt he should be able to have that option, passing the Michigan Medicinal Marijuana Act on a ballot referendum in 2008. The law allows Casias to carry a medical card and to have up to 2.5 ounces of marijuana, purchased from licensed caregivers, who can legally grow 12 plants at one time.

Furthermore, the law states that people like Casias cannot be discriminated against for medicating legally with marijuana: From the law:

> Sec. 4. (a) A qualifying patient who has been issued and possesses a registry identification card shall not be subject to arrest, prosecution, or penalty in any manner, or denied any right or privilege, *including but not limited to civil penalty or disciplinary action by a business or occupational or professional licensing board or bureau, for the medical use of marihuana in accordance with this act*, provided that the qualifying patient possesses an amount of marihuana that does not exceed 2.5 ounces of usable marihuana, and, if the qualifying patient has not specified that a primary caregiver will be allowed under state law to cultivate marihuana for the qualifying patient, 12 marihuana plants kept in an enclosed, locked facility. Any incidental amount of seeds, stalks, and unusable roots shall also be allowed under state law and shall not be included in this amount.

"We think it's illegal to fire somebody for using medical marijuana in accordance with state law," charges Dan Korobkin, an attorney for the Michigan American Civil Liberties Union, which appears prepared to take on a fight with Wal-Mart. "Firing somebody for doing something that is within the law when they have been a model employee . . . it's immoral and wrong."

Wal-Mart Holds the Power

This troubling story has drawn swift support for Casias, and similar condemnations from strangers who likely sense some of his acute vulnerability in themselves. He says he is grateful for all of the outreach, but he is mostly concerned with taking care of his family. "There is really no other job for me to get," he said, telling me he had once aspired to store manager, even district manager at Wal-Mart.

"Just look around Michigan—there are no jobs. Wal-Mart is one of the only places employing people," he told me matter-of-factly.

"I can't pay the bills. Everytime I look at (my children) . . . you know there are things children need—clothes, food, a roof over their heads. It's expensive."

When he speaks about his former employer is it heartbreaking—there is no malice, but instead a sad confusion about the betrayal. It happened so fast, his apparent fall from grace and re-emergence as a movement martyr, that he has cried openly and is visibly shaken. Why not? He's not made of China plastic—his fate now, being jobless and swimming in unpaid medical bills, is clearly uncertain.

"I have so many hospital bills in collections. I'm trying to make payments. I finally get on health care and then I lose my job. The thing I don't really understand is that I tried my best. I don't think I deserve to get fired. I never harmed anybody, I never harmed any customers or associates, never in the whole time," he said.

A Partial Turnaround

Wal-Mart was so righteous in its move to sever all ties with this heretofore loyal associate, that it initially tried to block his access to unemployment benefits, too. "This is not acceptable," said Mike Meno of the Washington-based Marijuana Policy Project, which launched a boycott of Wal-Mart, shortly after the story broke. "This is a guy with kids. Not only is this shameful neglect and immoral, but it is potentially illegal."

Perhaps sensing the growing public outrage (and with an eye towards pre-empting civil action) the company now says it will not object to Casias collecting unemployment. However, Wal-Mart has no plans to hire him back, recently releasing this statement to the media:

"Employee drug testing has gone too far."

In states such as Michigan, where prescriptions for marijuana can be obtained, an employer can still enforce a policy that requires termination of employment following a positive drug screen. We believe our policy complies with the law, and we support decisions based on the policy.

Fee-Fi-Fo-Fum

That Wal-Mart is drawing a line in the sand against medical marijuana—which has been legalized in 14 states and is being debated by at least 16 others today—shouldn't come as any surprise. Sure, we are outraged by the seeming cold-bloodedness in the company's statement that it is "sympathetic to Mr. Casias' condition," the company at once living up to the long-spun image of the Death Star, grinding up new communities and dispatching misfit employees with detached laser precision.

But the vision of Sam Walton, founder of this empire based out of Bentonville, Arkansas, has never really wavered from the "Gospel of Christian free enterprise," which is more than not tailor made for the Republican social conservative agenda in Washington. In fact, until this year, Wal-Mart stores and the Walton family had long been generous supporters of Republican federal candidates and causes (they've been spreading the love now that Democrats are in charge). The corporation often wades into political minefields—at one point being accused of openly telling its employees to vote Republican in the 2008 presidential election.

All this to say, that as Republicans in Washington have largely amassed on the side of prohibition where marijuana is concerned, my guess is that Wal-Mart, at least in ideological principle, has likely already shifted there too, along with lawmakers like Sen. Tom Coburn (R-OK), who thinks most medical marijuana users are fakers, and Rep. Mark Souder (R-IN), who says "smoked marijuana, along with tobacco and alcohol, is the gateway drug for all other drug abuse."

Making Casias an Example

If that is the case, then Casias' firing—aside from a cynical move to avoid taking on the poor guy's medical costs—could be making a 29-year-old cancer patient with two young children an example; an opening salvo in a nationwide fight to resist new medical marijuana protections at all costs.

"I think it is very significant that one of the largest employers in the United States—if not the largest—appears to be taking a position that employees have to choose between their jobs, which they do well, and treating their disease and treating their pain in a way that is recognized under the law. Especially in Michigan, which has the highest unemployment rate in the country now . . . it's irrational and it's illegal," said Korobkin.

The Michigan Medical Marijuana Association recently organized a protest rally in front of the Battle Creek store. Unfortunately, Wal-Mart typically weathers such public displays pretty well. Except of course, when protests are coming from the Right, then it tends to give in skittishly.

A Welcome Battle

Greg Francisco of the MMMA says Wal-Mart is just the razor-edged peak of a potential iceberg facing the Michigan medical marijuana movement in the coming months and years. Several towns and cities have filed ordinances to derail the law, despite popular support and more than 20,000 residents who have applied for medical cards. But he welcomes the fight, which will likely reflect other skirmishes across the country as medical marijuana becomes more legalized, more culturally accepted (a whopping 44 percent of Americans are now in favor of legalizing marijuana altogether) and more threatening to the social conservative status quo.

"I think collectively, it has a positive effect," Francisco said, because the movement supporters get more publicity the more they have to crowd town meetings to raise a stink. So far they're waiting for a "test case" to go full throttle against what they say are illegal restrictions being placed on patients under new ordinances.

Casias doesn't necessarily feel comfortable being a test case, nor a David, though he might very well be, in a courtroom, or at the very least, the court of public opinion.

VIEWPOINT 6

> *"Employers [are] in a difficult position,*
> *trying to accommodate state laws*
> *on medical marijuana use while . . .*
> *enforc[ing] . . . company drug-use*
> *policies that are based on federal law."*

At Work, a Drug Dilemma

Stephanie Simon

Stephanie Simon is a reporter for the Wall Street Journal. *In the following viewpoint, she contends that the wave of labor issues unleashed by the legalization of medical marijuana reveals that employers need a comprehensive policy on how to treat employees who use medical marijuana. In many cases, Simon points out, employers are caught between state and federal laws regarding the drug. She also argues that more sophisticated testing would help employers determine whether employees were high on the job or whether the drug had been ingested hours before they reported to work, but such advanced tests are very expensive for most employers.*

As you read, consider the following questions:

1. According to Simon, marijuana is a Schedule I drug on par with what two illegal substances?

2. What two states does Simon say have passed laws that dictate that most employers may not penalize individuals for using medical marijuana?
3. At what level of THC in the blood is a marijuana user considered high, according to Robert Lantz?

An employee recently approached Josh Ward, an executive at a Denver plumbing company, with a question he never thought he'd hear.

Her husband, the employee said, is a state-registered medical marijuana patient. Could she buy his marijuana with her company-provided flexible spending account?

"We were like, 'Whoa!'" Mr. Ward said.

Mr. Ward did a bit of research and quickly told the employee no. Her account, funded with pretax dollars, is regulated by the Internal Revenue Service and cannot be used to purchase a drug that's illegal under federal statutes, even if Colorado treats it as a legitimate medication.

The employee, whom the firm would not make available for comment, didn't press it, Mr. Ward said. Still, the issue made him uneasy. "It's a big can of worms," said Mr. Ward, vice president of Applewood Plumbing, Heating & Electric.

Employers from coast to coast are facing similar dilemmas. Many are closely watching a pending lawsuit against Wal-Mart Stores Inc. in Michigan. An employee who used medical marijuana was fired by the retailer after a positive drug test on the job.

Fourteen states and the District of Columbia have laws or constitutional amendments that allow patients with certain medical conditions such as cancer, glaucoma or chronic pain, to use marijuana without fear of prosecution. The Obama administration has directed federal prosecutors not to bring criminal charges against marijuana users who follow their states' laws.

But that can put employers in a difficult position, trying to accommodate state laws on medical marijuana use while at times having to enforce federal rules or company drug-use policies that are based on federal law.

"It's certainly an issue that's coming up regularly," said Danielle Urban, an attorney with Fisher & Phillips, a national labor and employment law firm. "Employers are between a rock and a hard place."

The federal government lists marijuana as a Schedule I drug on par with LSD or synthetic heroin. Employers can fire, or refuse to hire, employees for using the drug without running afoul of the Americans with Disabilities Act or any other federal anti-discrimination statute, said Christopher Kuczynski, assistant legal counsel with the U.S. Equal Employment Opportunity Commission.

State laws vary considerably. The state Supreme Courts in Oregon, California and Montana and the Washington Court of Appeals have all ruled that employers have a right to fire medical-marijuana patients for using the drug. The medical-marijuana laws in Rhode Island and Maine state that most employers may not penalize individuals solely because of their status as marijuana patients.

In Michigan, the law states that registered patients shall not be "denied any right or privilege" or face disciplinary action at work because they use pot. The only exception: Employers do have the right to terminate workers who use marijuana on site or come to work high.

But determining if a worker is impaired on the job can be difficult.

Sean Short, a 25-year-old college student, was injured last fall while taking pictures of skiers in Breckenridge, Colo., for his employer, an event photographer. Mr. Short says that, at the time, he was using marijuana in compliance with Colorado law to ease pain from a back injury.

He says he was not high when a skier smashed into him on the job, fracturing his shoulder. Mr. Short says he was required by his employer to take a urine drug screen after the accident.

He flunked. He then gave managers his medical-marijuana card. "They said, 'Sorry, we're terminating you,'" Mr. Short said.

His employer did not return calls seeking comment.

Mr. Short says he's now reluctant to apply for any job requiring a drug test. "I can have a college degree. I can be well-spoken and intelligent," he said. "But as long as I'm a 'druggie,' I'm going to be discriminated against."

Sophisticated tests can measure the amount of THC, the active ingredient in marijuana, in blood samples taken within four to six hours of ingestion. Users are generally considered high at a level of five nanograms of THC per milliliter of blood, said Robert Lantz, director of Rocky Mountain Instrumental Laboratories, a drug-testing facility in Fort Collins, Colo.

Such precise tests require expensive instruments. Dr. Lantz's lab charges $450 for a single blood test; his bulk discount rate is $200 per test. Many employers use far cheaper, less sensitive urine screens. At OnSite Medical Testing, a lab in Greenwood Village, Colo., a basic urine test costs $35, or $25 for bulk clients.

The typical urine screen can detect the presence of metabolized THC compounds, but can't determine when the marijuana was ingested or in what quantities, Dr. Lantz said.

Advocates of legalized marijuana say they would never insist that workers be allowed to use the drug on duty. "No one thinks you should be able to get stoned and go to work, obviously," said Keith Stroup, legal counsel for the national advocacy group NORML. Still, Mr. Stroup argues that, absent clear signs of impairment, employers should trust workers who have valid medical-marijuana-registration cards to take the drug responsibly.

Too dangerous, some employers say. At Hoffman Construction Co. in Portland, Ore., cannabis has been implicated more than any other drug in workplace accidents resulting in injury or property damage, said Dan Harmon, a vice president.

Any move to permit off-duty drug use raises "real safety concerns," Mr. Harmon said. His firm doesn't accept medical-marijuana cards, he said. To do so would be "disastrous."

Employers and medical-marijuana patients are hoping the Michigan lawsuit can bring some clarity to the situation.

Joseph Casias, who says he uses medical marijuana to ease pain from an inoperable brain tumor, sued Wal-Mart in a state court in June, saying the retailer was wrong to fire him from his job as an inventory manager in Battle Creek, Mich., after he tested positive for marijuana.

Mr. Casias, who is represented by the American Civil Liberties Union, says he uses cannabis on his oncologist's advice and in compliance with Michigan law. The 30-year-old father of two says he takes the drug at night and has never come to work high. But last November, he failed a drug test that was administered as a matter of company policy after he twisted his knee on the job.

A Wal-Mart spokesman called the case "unfortunate" and the decision to fire Mr. Casias "difficult." But, he said: "As more states allow this treatment, employers are left without any guidelines except the federal standard. In these cases, until further guidance is available, we will always default to what we believe is the safest environment for our associates and customers."

Periodical and Internet Sources Bibliography

The following articles have been selected to supplement the diverse views presented in this chapter.

Ian Danielson	"Medical Marijuana and Driving: A Policy Memo to Colorado Legislators," *Huffington Post*, September 8, 2011. www.huffing tonpost.com.
Denver Post	"Federal Government Clouds Medical Marijuana in Colorado," October 5, 2011.
Clay Dillow	"Medical Marijuana Laws Shown to Reduce Traffic Fatalities," *Popular Science*, November 20, 2011.
Les Rosan	"Case Illustrates Flaws in Medical Marijuana Law," *Morning Sun* (Central MI), February 19, 2011.
Kevin A. Sabet	"Does Medical Marijuana Really Reduce Alcohol Crash Fatalities?," *Huffington Post*, December 5, 2011. www.huffingtonpost.com.
Buck Sexton	"Should Medical Marijuana Users Lose Gun Rights?," *The Blaze*, September 29, 2011.
Christopher Shea	"Do Medical Marijuana Laws Reduce Highway Deaths?," *Wall Street Journal*, November 30, 2011.
Jordan Smith	"Medi-Pot Patient Sues Wal-Mart," *Austin Chronicle*, July 12, 2010.
Maia Szalavitz	"Why Medical Marijuana Laws Reduce Traffic Deaths," *Time*, December 2, 2011.
Townhall	"Medical Marijuana Users Fight for Gun Rights," April 4, 2011. www .townhall.com
Scott Willoughby	"ATF Goes Too Far in Restricting Medical-Pot Patients' Gun Rights," *Denver Post*, October 5, 2011.

For Further Discussion

Chapter 1

1. Should medical marijuana be legal? Read opposing viewpoints by Daniel J. Pfeifer and the Drug Enforcement Administration (DEA) to inform your opinion.
2. Americans for Safe Access contends that cannabis should be reclassified. Tom Strode asserts that the US government is right not to reclassify it. After reading both perspectives, which viewpoint makes the more persuasive argument? Why and how?
3. Many policy makers and officials worry that legalizing medical marijuana sends the wrong message to young people. Read viewpoints by the *Christian Science Monitor* and Mary Pat Angelini. What kind of message do you think legalizing medical marijuana sends to young people?

Chapter 2

1. The viewpoints in this chapter examine the question of whether medical marijuana is beneficial for society. Read each viewpoint carefully and then present your opinion on the question. Use information from one or more of the viewpoints to support your argument.
2. Does marijuana have medicinal value? The Center for Health and Pharmaceutical Law and Policy of the Seton Hall University School of Law wrote a brief arguing that it does. In his viewpoint, John Hoeffel outlines the government's statement that marijuana does not have a proven medicinal value. Does the Seton Hall viewpoint make a persuasive case? Why or why not?

Chapter 3

1. How should medical marijuana dispensaries be regulated? Tristan Scott maintains that there needs to be more

regulation of medical marijuana dispensaries. In his viewpoint, Brian Doherty contends that the extensive regulation of these dispensaries is discriminatory and reveals unfair treatment of medical marijuana. What is your opinion on the matter? Use information from the viewpoints to support your position.

2. Many veterans and mental health professionals are pushing for more research on the use of marijuana for US veterans suffering from post-traumatic stress disorder. John Grant supports this view. Brian Vastag points to a number of problems with this idea. How do you think the US government should proceed on this issue? How can many of the problems Vastag underlines be addressed?

Chapter 4

1. How should drugged drivers be treated? Read viewpoints by Ralph Vartabedian and Paul Armentano to illuminate the debate. Present your views on the subject.

2. In many states that have legalized the use of medical marijuana, there has been a debate over gun rights. Peter Bella maintains that medical marijuana users should be barred from purchasing firearms. Phillip Smith argues that gun owners should not have to give up their rights if they use medical marijuana. Which position do you agree with and why?

3. Another emerging controversy with the use of medical marijuana is labor rights. Should companies be able to fire employees who use medical marijuana? Read viewpoints by Kelley Vlahos and Stephanie Simon to inform your answer.

Organizations to Contact

The editors have compiled the following list of organizations concerned with the issues debated in this book. The descriptions are derived from materials provided by the organizations. All have publications or information available for interested readers. The list was compiled on the date of publication of the present volume; names, addresses, phone and fax numbers, and e-mail and Internet addresses may change. Be aware that many organizations take several weeks or longer to respond to inquiries, so allow as much time as possible.

American Civil Liberties Union (ACLU)

125 Broad Street, 18th Floor
New York, NY 10004
(212) 549-2500
website: www.aclu.org

The American Civil Liberties Union (ACLU) is a national organization that works to protect the rights of individuals and communities as prescribed by the US Constitution. It lobbies Congress to pass legislation protecting civil liberties; employs lawyers to fight discrimination and injustice in court; and organizes activists, volunteers, and other organizations to protest the violation of civil liberties. The ACLU has also been very active in the fight for marijuana law reform, and has worked extensively to protect the rights of patients using legal medical marijuana.

American Medical Association (AMA)

515 N. State Street
Chicago, IL 60654
(800) 621-8335
website: www.ama-assn.org

The American Medical Association (AMA) is an association of physicians that works to "promote the art and science of medicine and the betterment of public health." One of the AMA's key aims is to help doctors better assist patients. The AMA supports more research into the medical uses of marijuana and has called the government to review the classification of cannabis as a Schedule I drug. The *Journal of the American Medical Association (JAMA)* is one of several journals published by AMA; others include *American Medical News, Virtual Mentor: A Forum for Medical Ethics*, and *AMA Wire*, a weekly newsletter that features commentary and breaking medical news.

Americans for Safe Access (ASA)

1322 Webster Street, Suite 402
Oakland, CA 94612
(510) 251-1856 • fax: (510) 510-2036
e-mail: info@safeaccessnow.org
website: www.safeaccessnow.org

Americans for Safe Access (ASA) is a membership organization devoted to ensuring safe and legal access to medical marijuana for eligible patients. ASA works to pass legislation legalizing medical marijuana through lobbying, cannabis education, and media outreach. ASA also monitors law enforcement efforts in states where marijuana is legal for medical purposes, working to defend the rights of patients and providers. ASA's recent campaigns and efforts are chronicled on the group's website, which also features a blog, forums, and information about available resources.

Drug Policy Alliance Network (DPA Network)

70 W. 36th Street, 16th Floor
New York, NY 10018
(212) 613-8020 • fax: (212) 613-8021
e-mail: nyc@drugpolicy.org
website: www.drugpolicy.org

The Drug Policy Alliance Network (DPA) is one of the leading organizations in the United States promoting alternative drug policies. The DPA advocates policies that reduce the harms of both drug misuse and drug prohibition and work to ensure that drug policies no longer arrest, incarcerate, disenfranchise, and otherwise harm millions of nonviolent people. The DPA seeks to influence the legislative process by opposing draconian and harmful initiatives and promoting sensible drug policy reforms. The group has been active in California's Propositions 5 and 36, reforming the Rockefeller Drug Laws in New York and the Safety First movement in New Jersey. The DPA has published several in-depth reports on various drugs and their effects on communities, drug policy, and legislative initiatives by experts in the field, which are available on its website.

Marijuana Policy Project (MPP)
236 Massachusetts Ave. NE, Suite 400
Washington, DC 20002
(202) 462-5747
e-mail: info@mpp.org
website: wwww.mpp.org

The Marijuana Policy Project (MPP) is an organization established to garner support for medical marijuana policies in the United States. The MPP lobbies for the legalization of medical marijuana and full legalization, works to raise awareness of the medical benefits of marijuana and the wrong-headedness of current marijuana policy, and garner favorable media coverage for medical marijuana laws and regulations. The MPP website features a range of information on the value of medical marijuana, including briefing reports, fact sheets, and commentary on the topic. It also includes a blog, video, press releases, and breaking news. The MPP publishes the *Marijuana Policy Report*, a newsletter that offers updates on ongoing efforts and campaigns.

Multidisciplinary Association for Psychedelic Studies (MAPS)
1215 Mission Street
Santa Cruz, CA 95060

(831) 429-6362 • fax: (831) 429-6370
e-mail: askmaps@maps.org
website: www.maps.org

The Multidisciplinary Association for Psychedelic Studies (MAPS) was founded in 1986 to work for the legalization of marijuana and psychedelic drugs to treat conditions like Post-Traumatic Stress Disorder (PTSD), chronic pain, depression, and anxiety. MAPS seeks to educate the public, media, legislators and policy makers, and medical professionals on the value of medical marijuana and funds scientific research into the medical benefits of marijuana and psychedelic drugs. Much of this research is accessible on the MAPS website. MAPS also sends out a monthly e-newsletter as well as the *MAPS Bulletin*, which is published three times a year.

National Organization for the Reform of Marijuana Laws (NORML)

1600 K Street NW, Mezzanine Level
Washington, DC 20006
(202) 483-5500 • fax: (202) 483-0057
e-mail: norml@norml.org
website: norml.org

The National Organization for the Reform of Marijuana Laws (NORML) is a nonprofit advocacy group founded in 1970 to lobby against harsh marijuana policies and laws. According to its mission statement, NORML aims to "move public opinion sufficiently to achieve the repeal of marijuana prohibition so that the responsible use of cannabis by adults is no longer subject to penalty." NORML acts to educate the public and media about marijuana and the benefits of marijuana reform and lobbies state and federal legislators to reform unfair marijuana laws. The NORML website provides a wealth of information on marijuana legislation and reform, as well as the issues associated with medical marijuana. It also features reports, fact sheets, commentaries and in-depth studies on important issues, a blog, and an e-newsletter.

Patients Out of Time (POT)

1472 Fish Pond Road
Howardsville, VA 24562
(434) 263-4484 • fax: (434) 263-6753
e-mail: patients@medicalcannabis.com
website: www.medicalcannabis.com

Patients Out of Time (POT) is a nonprofit educational organization that aims to educate health care and medical professionals, patients, and the public about the medicinal benefits of cannabis. It works to support the legalization of medical marijuana across the country. POT hosts a conference every few years for caregivers and health care professionals to disseminate information and breakthroughs in the field. The POT website features information on federal and state laws on medical marijuana, the most recent research on the drug, and patient testimonials and resources. It also provides a comprehensive overview of the drug's medicinal value and therapeutic uses.

Students for Sensible Drug Policy (SSDP)

1317 F Street NW, Suite 501
Washington, DC 20004
(202) 393-5280 • fax: (202) 293-8344
e-mail: ssdp@ssdp.org
website: ssdp.org

Students for a Sensible Drug Policy (SSDP) is "an international grassroots network of students who are concerned about the impact drug abuse has on our communities, but who also know that the War on Drugs is failing our generation and our society." SSDP mobilizes young people to participate in the democratic process to push for sensible drug laws and to change harsh, counterproductive existing drug laws. The SSDP views marijuana as a public health issue and supports the use of medical marijuana for patients who need it. One of the organization's key aims is to generate a productive, realistic conversation on the failure of the War on Drugs and the effect of unfair drug policy on regular citizens, communities, the US legal system, and the future.

US Department of Veterans Affairs (VA)

810 Vermont Ave. NW
Washington, DC 20420
(800) 827-1000
website: www.va.gov

Established in 1930, the US Department of Veterans Affairs (once known as the Veterans Administration, or VA) is the government department that coordinates and administers veterans programs, including health services, disability compensation, educational and vocational programs, home loans, life insurance, survivors' benefits, and burial remuneration. One of its most important responsibilities is the VA health system, which supervises facilities that offer a wide range of medical, surgical, and rehabilitative care for veterans. In the VA health care system, there are 171 medical centers; 350 outpatient, community, and outreach clinics; and 126 nursing home care units. The VA provides a link to recent congressional testimony, speeches, brochures, fact sheets, official forms, manuals, handbooks, updates, and videos on its website. The agency also publishes the *VAnguard*, the bimonthly magazine that explores issues relevant to veterans' concerns.

US Drug Enforcement Administration (DEA)

Mailstop: AES, 8701 Morrissette Drive
Springfield, VA 22152
(202) 307-1000
website: www.dea.gov

The US Drug Enforcement Administration (DEA) is a department of the US Department of Justice that is focused on enforcing the nation's drug laws and reducing the amount of illegal drugs available to consumers in the United States. The DEA investigates and prosecutes drug gangs and smugglers; collaborates with legislators and policy makers to formulate an effective and comprehensive drug policy; and coordinates with other countries and international organizations to confront international drug smuggling. The DEA is responsible for enforcing federal marijuana laws and determining the federal approach to the treatment of state medical marijuana policies. The DEA publishes *Dateline DEA*, a biweekly electronic newsletter that provides updates on recent campaigns and new policies, as well as *Speaking Out Against Drug Legalization*.

Bibliography of Books

Greg Campbell

Pot, Inc.: Inside Medical Marijuana, America's Most Outlaw Industry. New York: Sterling, 2012.

Isaac Campos

Home Grown: Marijuana and the Origins of Mexico's War on Drugs. Chapel Hill: University of North Carolina Press, 2012.

Wendy Chapkis and Richard J. Webb

Dying to Get High: Marijuana as Medicine. New York: New York University Press, 2008.

Mitch Earleywine, ed.

Pot Politics: Marijuana and the Costs of Prohibition. Oxford, UK: Oxford University Press, 2007.

Steve Elliot

The Little Black Book of Marijuana: The Essential Guide to the World of Cannabis. White Plains, NY: Peter Pauper Press, 2011.

Erin P. Finley

Fields of Combat: Understanding PTSD Among Veterans of Iraq and Afghanistan. Ithaca, NY: ILR Press, 2011.

Matthew Gavin Frank

Pot Farm. Lincoln: University of Nebraska Press, 2012.

Madelon Lubin Frankel

Truth, Lies, and Public Health: How We Are Affected When Science and Politics Collide. Westport, CT: Praeger, 2007.

Jeff S. Gauer	*The Toke Book! The MMJ Guide for New Smokers: Maximizing the Benefits of Medical Marijuana Through Smoking.* Colorado Springs, CO: Work-Playground Press, 2011.
John Geluardi	*Cannabiz: The Explosive Rise of the Medical Marijuana Industry.* Sausalito, CA: Polipoint Press, 2010.
Julie Holland, ed.	*The Pot Book: A Complete Guide to Cannabis: Its Role in Medicine, Politics, Science, and Culture.* Rochester, VT: Park Street Press, 2010.
Leslie L. Iverson	*The Science of Marijuana.* New York: Oxford University Press, 2008.
Albert T. Johnson, ed.	*Medical Marijuana and Marijuana Use.* New York: Nova Science, 2009.
Brigid M. Kane	*Marijuana.* New York: Chelsea House, 2011.
Martin A. Lee	*Smoke Signals: A Social History of Marijuana—Medical, Recreational & Scientific.* New York: Scribner, 2012.
Jeffrey Matthew London	*How the Use of Marijuana Was Criminalized and Medicalized, 1906–2004: A Foucaltian History of Legislation in America.* Lewiston, NY: Edwin Mellen Press, 2009.

John McCabe — *Marijuana & Hemp: History, Uses, Laws, and Controversy.* Santa Monica, CA: Carmania Books, 2011.

Kayla Morgan — *Legalizing Marijuana.* Edina, MN: ABDO, 2011.

Gary Potter, Tom Decorte, and Martin Bouchard — *World Wide Weed: Global Trends in Cannabis Cultivation and Its Control.* Burlington, VT: Ashgate, 2010.

Trish Regan — *Joint Ventures: Inside America's Almost Legal Marijuana Industry.* Hoboken, NJ: Wiley, 2011.

Andrea S. Rojas, ed. — *Marijuana: Uses, Effects and the Law.* Hauppauge, NY: Nova Science, 2011.

Mark Haskell Smith — *The Heart of Dankness: Underground Botanists, Outlaw Farmers, and the Race for the Cannabis Cup.* New York: Broadway, 2012.

Matthew Stolick — *Otherwise Law-Abiding Citizens: A Scientific and Moral Assessment of Cannabis Use.* Lanham, MD: Lexington Books, 2009.

Index